Nativities and Passions

Nativities and Passions

Words for Transformation

Martin L. Smith, SSJE

COWLEY PUBLICATIONS
Cambridge ✦ Boston
Massachusetts

Published in the United States of America by Cowley Publications, a division of the Society of St. John the Evangelist. No portion of this book may be reproduced, stored in or introduced into a retrieval system, or transmitted, in any form or by any means—including photocopying—without the prior written permission of Cowley Publications, except in the case of brief quotations embodied in critical articles and reviews.

Library of Congress Cataloging-in-Publication Data:
Smith, Martin Lee.
  Nativities and passions: words for transformation / Martin L. Smith.
      p.   cm.
  Includes bibliographical references.
  ISBN 1-56101-116-9 (alk. paper)
  1. Sermons, American. 2. Episcopal Church—Sermons. 3. Anglican Communion—Sermons. I. Title.
  BX5937.S58N38   1995
  252'.03—dc20   95-35008
                                                       CIP

Scripture quotations are from the *New Revised Standard Version* of the Bible, © 1989 by the Division of Christian Education of the National Council of the Churches of Christ in the USA. Used by permission. All rights reserved.

Grateful acknowledgment is given to the following:
Many Rivers Press for permission to quote from *Where Many Rivers Meet* by David Whyte; Random House, Inc. for permission to quote from *W. H. Auden: Collected Poems*; and Macmillan for permission to quote from the *Collected Poems* of W. B. Yeats.

Editor: Cynthia Shattuck
Copyeditor and Designer: Vicki Black
Cover Design: Vicki Black

This book is printed on recycled, acid-free paper and was produced in the United States of America.

Cowley Publications
28 Temple Place
Boston, Massachusetts 02111

To my mother and stepfather,
Pamela and William Horne,
with love and gratitude

Contents

Foreword

To prepare this collection of sermons for publication I chose a certain few days after Easter and withdrew to a small cabin in the woods near Emery House, our retreat center at West Newbury, Massachusetts. In one of those coincidences that constantly make us wonder about the way grace permeates everyday life, the gospel reading for the day I completed the task was the story of the feeding of the five thousand from the gospel of John. Jesus told his disciples, "Gather up the fragments left over, so that nothing may be lost."

These words are a great encouragement to help overcome a preacher's diffidence in collecting sermons. It is easy to feel that sermons are by their very nature ephemeral, tied to occasions. The written texts even seem like "left-overs" from a meal, something that won't keep. The gospel story shows Jesus full of strange solicitude for the left-overs from the mysterious feast on the hillside. In John's gospel this concern seems to be an expression of Jesus' confidence that "this is the will of him who sent me, that I should lose nothing of all that he has given me."

Fragments are not to be despised. It is the work of Jesus to gather everything together, and ultimately nothing is to be left out or left behind. In John's gospel Jesus' words "are spirit and life." And because he goes to the Father, the disciples will do works even greater than his; certainly their words may be like his in having an enduring power to nourish as "fruit that will last."

As I have gathered up these fragments of preaching I have found myself praying lines from the earliest eucharistic prayer we have, found in the *Didache*, a Christian handbook contemporary with John's gospel:

As this bread broken into fragments
  was scattered over the hillside
    and then brought together into one,
so let your Church be gathered together
    from the ends of the earth into your kingdom,
  for yours is the power through Jesus Christ for ever.

Sermons are bread broken into fragments, the good news divided up into helpings. Can they be brought together again into one? If they are collected together will they make a unity, a unity that points to the unifying and attractive power of God, the Center of all?

Leafing through many sermons from the last fifteen years I was reminded of an extraordinary experience I had in this very cabin one evening late in the fall of 1979. I set apart a few days for retreat to take stock of the great change that had taken place in my life, having transferred a few months earlier from the English branch of the Society of Saint John the Evangelist to the American branch. This crossing of the Atlantic seemed to be giving my life a completely new start. At nightfall I became aware of a kind of bodily restlessness unlike anything I had ever felt. Then suddenly I moved what sticks of furniture there were to the walls and to my amazement started to dance in the firelight. I have never danced; I had no experience to go on. And this was not just random dancing. What my body was doing was dancing the story of my life up to this point. After about four hours of intense movement I fell into a deep sleep.

The following day was one of amazement. How did my body know how to move like that? And how did it remember so much of my life, without being prompted by thought? It was an intense experience of what Walt Whitman in *Democratic Vistas* calls the "miracle of miracles...a thought that rises, independent, lifted out from all else, calm, like the stars, shining eternal. This is the thought of identity—yours for you, as mine for me." Now, fifteen years later, in putting together this collection of sermons I realize how there is an inevitable unity to them simply because they have emerged from my own life and experience and prayer. This is recollection, quite personal recollection; these sermons are saturated with memories of my own struggles and experiences of gift and transformation.

Recollection in solitude can be the occasion of an intense awareness of community; making this collection has made me aware again of how central to the Christian mystery is the experience of the social nature of our personhood, the social nature of God as Trinity. Editing these sermons has been a vivid experience of remembering all the members of the communities and settings in which I have been preaching over these years. Thus there is another kind of unity underlying a collection of sermons, the unity of common experience, the unity given by many conversations within the body of Christ and the human family. There are things we know as a community that we might not know as individuals.

As I have pondered some of these sermons and asked myself again what right I had to say many of the things in them, the answer has come to me that it is by virtue of the conversations of which I have been a part. This preaching arises from inner conversation with a vast range of men and women. There are saints, poets, writers, theologians, and philosophers here who have spoken to me through their writings. In these sermons there are signs everywhere of my teachers, those who have shared their religious experience with me in the context of retreats and spiritual direction, and very significantly, the brothers of my own community. Most of the sermons themselves are episodes in a continuous preaching conversation with a remarkable congregation that gathers not only on Sunday, but also every Tuesday afternoon at the monastery for the eucharist. This congregation is on a heartfelt spiritual quest. Its members call for depth, and it is a remarkable privilege to participate in the many-sided conversation which is the preaching life of our monastery.

The coherence of this collection is largely due to the skill of Cynthia Shattuck, editor of Cowley Publications, a colleague and friend for whom my affection and esteem continues to grow. She has been assisted most perceptively by Karen Fraioli, and I am very grateful to both of them.

This book has also given me the chance to work as an author with the Cowley staff and to witness their skill and dedication firsthand. I want to thank Vicki Black for her elegant book design and cover, Jennifer Hopcroft for her work in publicity, and Charles Maynard for selling my books with such enthusiasm.

The title *Nativities and Passions* expresses the concerns that constantly play through my mind, heart, and soul as a preacher. Passion must be the word most constantly found on my lips whenever I have the opportunity to voice what truly matters to me. The passion of the God of desire, the evoking of passionate desire for God. The suffering of God for us, and the suffering we have to undergo to break through to the experience of liberated desire. As for nativities—preaching, as well as spiritual direction and teaching, is about helping to bring to birth. We do not marshal the ranks of fully-grown beliefs and mature experience. We are supposed to be in at the birth, to help insight and discovery and choice breathe and be fed at the beginning. What is born then takes on a life of its own in the believer's care; our work may be over at the beginning.

Nativities

Would You Like to Hold Him?

Christmas Eve, at the monastery

I was coming out of the new art gallery in Atlanta shortly after it opened when I overheard a small, middle-aged man, obviously in from the country, say to his wife in a low, disapproving tone, "So many pictures of *her*...." Of course, you know who he meant, because there *are* a lot of pictures of *her*, Mary. There seems no end to them: pictures of her feeding Jesus at her breast, holding him as he stands proudly on her knee, gazing down at him, holding him to her cheek, proudly enthroned with him like Wisdom herself, pregnant with him.

So many images, so many styles and titles, so many associations with so many places: Our Lady of Walsingham, of Vladimir. There are glorious icons, Renaissance masterpieces, and local primitives like the one we had at the back of our parish church in England. Because the naïve artist had heard the story read without regard to punctuation, he depicted Mary and Joseph lying in the manger as well as the babe!

Fortunately we will have all of eternity to search out the limitless meanings of all these aspects of Mary and her child. In our earthly lifetime most of us will only scratch the surface of the truth and meaning bound up in all these varied representations. The best we can do is pray our way into them one by one.

This year one image of Mary and her child has stayed with me and I want to tell you about it. It is a simple limestone statue in the chapel of Burford Priory in England, a small house of Anglican Benedictines. Mary is standing and is holding the baby in such a way that he is facing us with his arms spread out, the back of his wrists against her shoulders. She is looking down, down at the top of his head, down toward us kneeling below.

I prayed silently before this statue for a whole week before I caught on; all I knew in my tiredness was that I needed to be there. But a few days ago I got out the photograph of the statue that I had taken, and what must be obvious to anyone with any sense struck me instantly for the first time. Jesus, the naked baby leaning against the body of Mary, has adopted the form he will take when they nail him naked to the cross. Mary holds him there, as she is going to again when she stands beneath the cross uniting her own will with his own self-offering.

If there is any image of the mother and child to stay with, this must be the one. We gladly flip through the hundred and one Madonnas and Marys of the Christmas cards, but we will not pray with them. Nothing sugared, nothing immaculate, nothing soft and soothing is of any use to us for that. But we can linger with this image because it tells us the truth, and only the truth can set us free. The truth is that this baby, like every baby, is born to die—but this baby, unlike every baby, is born to die for the sins of all. The death this baby is born for is the answer to the outrage of evil. The wound which will be opened in his side will be the inexhaustible source of healing for everything that evil has ruined.

It is an open secret that the inmost experience of many at Christmas is soreness of heart, soreness at the bitter sufferings of the world, the trapped in Bosnia, the starving and ruined in Somalia, soreness at the banal but frightful pain harbored in our own families. A quick fix of Yuletide cheer and a day's hilarity, and then there is the morning after the night before. The mystery expressed in this statue of Mary and her child is not 'the quick fix, the momentary relief of turning away "from the sorrow that makes today today, and tomorrow tomorrow." Mary asks us to take a long look at her baby, his arms stretched out on the cross of her body. Look, she tells us, this is God coming into the world to keep us company in the worse that can befall us. This is love in crucified companionship coming to bear the world's pain in pierced hands.

In some way I cannot describe or explain, Mary appears to be on the point of handing her baby over into our arms. Some images of Mary have her so wrapped up in her child that we are left simply looking on in wonderment at the mystery of motherhood. But in this statue she is the very image of open-handedness: "Here, would you like to hold him?"

This mother's question and offer takes us to the heart of the celebration of Christmas. It is as if Mary says to us, "Here, take him. You can hold him if you like." Of course, many of us do not know whether we would like to hold him or not. Couldn't we just look? But there is something about the motherhood of Mary that is not merely openhanded. Mary really says to us, "My baby is as much yours as he is mine. Jesus is of all and for all. He belongs to you as much as to me. Let me hand him over to you."

It is not so easy, after all, to take Jesus into our arms if Jesus is who they say he is. If Jesus is God with us, the very embodiment of God, then the baby in our arms puts us in a ridiculous position. We have God in our arms! We are holding God, and the worst that God can do there is wet us by accident or burp! This is absurd—surely God is all-powerful and fearful. How can you be afraid of a baby?

We cannot hold onto our dread of God and still hold baby 'Emmanuel in our arms. Either one or the other. This is why Christmas is so full of penitence and judgment. We are so attached to our fear of God. We are so convinced that God is menacing, though we say bravely that he is love. We are so sure that God's closeness would be invasive, overwhelming; so convinced that he is dangerous, that we must keep our distance to play safe. All this comes under judgment at Christmas when Mary says, "Here is the God you are so afraid of. Will you take him in your arms?" To do so, we have to let go of our fear.

From the earliest days Mary has been revered as the place of transformation and change. Listen to the words of the great theologian of Syria, Ephraim of Edessa, who wrote his theology in the form of chorales to be sung by a choir of women, praising Mary as the place where God is transformed.

> Your mother is a cause for wonder: the Lord entered her
> and became a servant; He who is the Word entered
> and became silent within her; thunder entered her
> and made no sound. There entered the Shepherd of all,
> and in her He became the Lamb,
>> bleating as He came forth.
> Your mother's womb has reversed the roles;
> the Establisher of all entered in his richness,
> but came forth poor; the Exalted One entered her,
> but came forth meek; the Splendrous One entered her
> but came forth having put on a lowly hue.
> The Mighty One entered, and put on insecurity
> from her womb; the Provisioner of all entered
> and experienced hunger. He who gives drink to all entered
> and experienced thirst; naked and stripped
> there came forth from her He who clothes all.

Today in the eucharist we celebrate together this self-emptying and abasement of God, confessing together with mingled embarrassment and relief that once again we have been getting God all wrong. How did we let it happen? But we did, didn't we? We started being afraid of God again. We had gotten used all over again to wanting to keep our distance from a God who scared us. And so we have to start all over again.

The word comes to us from the angels, who patiently take us back to the beginning with their first words to Mary, "Fear not!" and their reassurance of the shepherds, "Don't be afraid." It will take us a long time to believe them, and when we come round to Easter next year the angels will still be saying to us what they said to the women at the tomb, "Don't be afraid." But we wouldn't need the angels if we heeded Mary. She hands us our God, new-born. We can hold our God in our arms. God has made our fear absurd. She says, "This is the one you were afraid of! Here, you can hold him if you like." Just as I am going to say to you in a few minutes, "Here, take him in the humble, harmless, homely form of bread. Take him, it really is him, but in a form that makes your fear absurd. Only love and gratitude and a broken pride overjoyed to be broken make sense here. There is room for all our feelings for God, but fear has been made out of date here."

We come together as we always do, and we celebrate the eucharist as we always have for the day of the nativity of Christ. It is simply the day, almost two thousand years ago, when being afraid of God became out of date.

Seek My Face

B ack in the 1950s you opened up the newspaper on the first of January certain to find the cartoonists trotting out the images of the little baby in diapers imprinted with the new year's numbers, and old Father Time with his hourglass and scythe. These secular symbols are already so threadbare that in comparison the scriptural image of today's liturgy, the Feast of the Holy Name, seems quite dramatic and still replete with meaning. Here the child held up before us is a real infant, and the figure with the sharp blade a real elder who cuts the flesh of the boy as the sign of the covenant with Abraham, while his parents give him his name. We are present at a fateful event: the newborn is becoming a person. And we are also persons, are becoming persons. This feast has to do with us. This becoming a person is what we would know the meaning of. Unless the year just beginning is the year we grasp more truly what we are growing into and toward, and what our becoming is for, it will be another of the wasted years.

Seven full days have passed since the birth of Jesus. A week of namelessness, a symbolic hiatus. The infant is only a newborn. Only on the eighth day does the trajectory of the child's human identity begin; he is acknowledged as a member of the community. He is inserted into its history, claimed by its tradition, and given a destiny within its future by naming. This name that bears his future is one that gathers up into a single sound the whole past experience and hope of his forebears and parents. *Yahweh Saves*. It is the name of the leader who took the desert wanderers into the promised land.

The feast is no longer called by its old name, the Feast of the Circumcision. This is partly, I suspect, out of the same kind of prudery that caused the choirboys in my church to snicker when that word was mentioned in any readings and the matrons in the pews to dart glances of disgusted reproof at them. On the other hand, the reason may lie deeper. Perhaps we are appalled to think about the radical givenness of identity that the irrevocable surgery on a helpless infant expresses so sharply—literally as a matter of flesh and blood. Before there is an I to choose, others choose and must mold and make me and do what calls me into life as a person in a particular community. Each of us is marked for life by the scandal of initial absolute dependence and vulnerability to the cutting edge of our situation. The persons we become can never dissolve or undo this givenness, though some of the wounds may heal and some of the blessings be lost.

No one can say that the classic pattern of the liturgy of Christmas (as opposed to commercial Yuletide) is light on the tragic side of human existence. It has its themes of the census, the exclusion from the inn, the martyrdom of Stephen, the massacre of the innocents, the flight into Egypt, and now this serious evocation of the wound of historical existence, of submission to the narrow way of becoming a unique person through utter dependence on others. But there is throughout the Christmas season an ambience of hope, a yes radiating from the face of Mary that prevails over the shadow. Mother and child smile in mutual recognition, in reciprocal joy. Many of us are captivated and allured by the mystery of Jesus' emerging self, summoned out of latency by his mother's gaze and care.

Recently I was at a party and spent a happy spell face-to-face with a smiling boy of about seven months. I smiled back, which is just what cunning nature intends. The child is wonderfully exercising his powers to recruit the attention so necessary for his survival. I was smiling both at him and his exercise of his winning power and my own recruitability, and at my funny celibate's knowledge of what goes on in the first year of life. The first three months, when the mouth serves as the cradle of perception, the receptive cavity by which the child incorporates the world. Then the mysterious shift toward the love object, the person present; at three months begins the universal smile in response to the presence of a face. The smile of this little boy at the sight of my face was, I couldn't help thinking, the most moving of mysteries. The fateful beginnings of the sense of identity and otherness, the start of the adventure of being a self with others, of I and thou, the agonizing search for an independence that is not isolation and a togetherness that does not absorb and consume.

As we contemplate in liturgy, icon, and prayer the face of Mary, we know we are in a mystery. This is the face that did something beside which Helen's feat of launching a thousand ships is insignificant. This face launched the movement of the Savior into both personhood and faith. This is the face in which Jesus felt the presence of a loving other, a presence and a sign of wholeness which orders the universe as safe enough for life.

We could do worse than begin the new year by paying loving attention to this crucible of personality, the face-to-face interaction of mother and child, Mary and Jesus, and the arms and face of Mary as primal originating sacrament of the faith and trust of Jesus. Return first to the face of the mother and then we can be ready to hear the words of the psalmist:

You speak in my heart and say, "Seek my face."
Your face, LORD, will I seek. (Psalm 27:11)

Once we are caught up in the struggles and gifts of the interpersonal adventure, then, if we are attentive to the voice of

God, we find ourselves drawn through, beyond, past, above the faces of our loves, to seek the Face.

The Psalter has left us one of the most pregnant images of life as a pilgrimage of men and women seeking the face of God. The climactic disclosures of the temple worship dramas were called by the term "beholding God's face" (sometimes translated "presence"). The psalms of pilgrimage are songs of seekers longing to be caught up in this gracious experience of the Lord's face shining upon them:

> At my vindication I shall see your face;
>> when I awake, I shall be satisfied,
>>> beholding your likeness. (Psalm 17:16)

The temple was destroyed but the songs live on; they sing of the human journey itself toward personal encounter with the unspeakably glorious God. The language is transfigured by use into a pointer to our destinies converging on personal union with God.

> For now we see in a mirror, dimly, but then we will see face to face. Now I know only in part; then I will know fully, even as I have been fully known. (1 Cor. 13:12)

"'Seek my face'...Your face, Lord, will I seek." Some of you know this dialogue by experience. You have felt the undertow, the tug, the summons to intimacy with God. You can remember the panic, the attempt at escape, evasion, denial. No, please, not this! Nothing so demanding or close; not this which throws into disarray the way I know myself. Not this risk of being touched so profoundly. Can't I go on being religious in my own little way? Some of you remember surrendering little by little, that it wasn't a matter of mystical flights but consent to the personal love of Jesus, consent to the fact that the Son and the Father are one, and that "the light of the knowledge of the glory of God" is found "in the face of Jesus Christ."

For those of us who remember this dialogue, it was a matter of looking Jesus in the face. We found ourselves knowing what St. Teresa meant when she told us, *"Mira que te mira....*Look at him looking at you lovingly and humbly." A change overtook us bit by bit and things couldn't be the same. We knew that this face-to-face prayer gave away the secret of who we are, who we are becoming, and who we shall all be. The change was conversion. Here in our community we see it day by day in one another and in those who come to stay for retreat. We see it as witnesses, sometimes as midwives, as brothers in discovery, sometimes just as holders of boxes of Kleenex.

On the other hand, there are those who know of the call "Seek my face" by hearsay only, or negatively, through a sense of wistfulness and lack, boredom with mere religion, or awareness of resistance and withholding. This face-to-face intimacy with God that is our end can be given by anticipation even now; the future can reach into the present by the free gift of God. It is an offer to all. We would be fools indeed not to reach out now for what is being offered to us by the love of God.

The Uncontrollable Mystery

Epiphany, at the Church of St. John the Evangelist, Boston

One of the many things that we do with language, as the philosopher Ludwig Wittgenstein pointed out, is to send it on holiday. From time to time we human beings release our language from the restrictions of technicality and everyday usage; we send it on holiday to play. And language does not merely return from its holiday refreshed, but also, from time to time, brings back some precious discovery from foreign parts.

Christmas is a time when most of us feel free to send language on holiday. We feel free to float in and out of legends and myths and ancient lore, while our carols have us virtually speaking in tongues as we warble "Lullee, lullay, Noel, *Gloria in excelsis Deo!*" It is to the poets we want to turn in that season. And if we listen carefully as the poets play with words at Christmas, we may find that "their right hand has taught them terrible things." E. M. Forster said that the most deep and terrible line written on the nativity is the last line of Yeats's poem, "The Magi":

Now as at all times I can see in the mind's eye,
In their stiff, painted clothes, the pale unsatisfied ones
Appear and disappear in the blue depth of the sky

With all their ancient faces like rain-beaten stones,
And all their helms of silver hovering side by side,
And all their eyes still fixed, hoping to find once more,
Being by Calvary's turbulence unsatisfied,
The uncontrollable mystery on the bestial floor.[1]

The uncontrollable mystery on the bestial floor. The magi mysteriously shimmer as faces in the sky, forever peering back behind Calvary to their encounter with the baby lying on the stable floor among oxen and asses, a revelation so mysterious that its depths still baffle them, ever preventing them from being satisfied.

The key to their dissatisfaction is the terrible word "uncontrollable." Magi were spiritual technicians. Their role was to assist people in getting control of their destinies through divinizing, augury, and horoscope. They offered means of controlling divine presences and forces through spells, charms, and rites. Human religiosity is about control. If the divine is close at hand, right here, then we can manipulate it. It is within our grasp, susceptible to our control. If, on the other hand, the divine is far away in a remote heaven, then we are on our own, and our religious practices serve just as well to calm our fears and put a spiritual gloss on our attempts to keep order.

What met the magi at Bethlehem was the mystery of divine creativity itself, which cannot be usurped or deflected; the uncontrollable mystery of God's sheer initiative, which cannot be bent or blocked. What met them was the mystery of suffering love, which cannot be bought or seduced, there, right there, lying on its back on the bestial floor. Here is the uncontrollable mystery of Love present in all its fullness as a vulnerable baby.

All at once their potions, their horoscopes, their charts and crystals, their incantations and secret lore collapse into nothing. So they unload onto the floor where the baby lies gazing at them their obsolete bag of tricks—the talismans of gold, the incense with which they fogged and scented their rituals, the myrrh they used for magic ointments. They let all these go in the presence of the uncontrollable mystery on the bestial floor.

St. Ignatius of Antioch wrote, just thirty years or so after Matthew's gospel was written, that the magi's star was the sign that with the coming of the Christ all magic was at an end. In the end, maybe the story of the magi jettisoning their bag of magic tricks at the manger is really our story. When we finally get to the bottom of our dread of God, our fear of Jesus, our evasion of the Spirit, our ambivalence about grace, we all seem to arrive at a moment of truth expressed in the simple words, "I'm afraid of letting go." All the scriptures seem to say to us then is, "That's right."

The Epiphany is a terrible scene, terrible to our need to be in control, because it invites letting go. Somehow the inmost meaning of it is bound up with the presence of the beasts, the animals; the uncontrollable mystery is on the *bestial* floor. The gospel mentions no beasts, but Christian art and poetry invariably and insistently include them. Look at your Christmas cards—the big-eyed donkeys in Ethiopian miniatures, the sheep and the camels in the old masters, the lowing cattle of our old carols. Remember the children carefully placing the creatures in the crèche. The baby lies among the beasts. Something deeply important is being signaled to us here. The One who has come among us is the Creator. The beasts look at the source of their life and beauty. This is the Source of life reembracing creation by joining creatures as a fellow-creature.

Poets grasp what embarrasses theologians. A wonderful poem, "On the Nativity of Our Lord and Saviour Jesus Christ," by the eighteenth-century Anglican poet Christopher Smart, sends language on holiday to learn from the birds:

Nature's decorations glisten
    Far above their usual trim;
Birds on box and laurel listen
    As so near the cherubs hymn....

Spinks and ouzels sing sublimely,
  "We too have a savior born";
Whiter blossoms burst untimely
  On the blest Mosaic thorn.

God all-bounteous, all creative,
  Whom no ills from good dissuade,
Is incarnate, and a native
  Of the very world he made.[2]

The Epiphany is a revelation of the sanctity of creaturehood. Being a creature in the living world of birds and beasts and reptiles is so holy that God could enter into creaturely life as a native of the very world he made and still be God. God could be at home on the bestial floor.

There is another meaning to this strange word, "bestial." It evokes our animality, our kinship with the beasts, a kinship now so clear to us as we decode the history of our evolution and see our behaviors mirrored in those of the birds and beasts. The word "bestial" pulls us down, reminds us of our enfleshedness, our sexuality, instinctuality, carnality, earthiness. The terrible scene of the stable—the baby still glistening from the juices of birth, surrounded by the cattle chewing their cud—wreaks havoc with our fearful need to keep God safely away from this flesh. But the Word was made flesh and dwelt among us to hallow—not deny—the realities of human life, to make holy—not to evaporate—our senses and sexuality. We thought religion was the law for controlling our animality and climbing above and beyond it to a higher plane, but now the uncontrollable mystery of sovereign Love comes right down onto the bestial floor and gives us an epiphany of flesh enlivened and transfigured, not repressed and trodden down.

Then there is the third and most awful implication of the word "bestial." It is a word used about human life when it becomes deranged and depraved, when it becomes enslaved and degraded, or when it goes berserk, crazed with blood-lust.

There is a bestial floor in the structure of human existence, the cellar where profiteers make hard-core porn movies that record actual slayings, where torturers ply their craft, where cruelty and violation pass unnoticed in ordinary life, and victims pass on their own fate in a mindless chain of abuse and suffering. It is a floor to which there are innumerable hidden stairs even in our cleanest suburbs.

In Yeats's poem the magi are unsatisfied by Calvary's turbulence and that is why they endlessly strain back to see the stable scene. Maybe that is their mistake. It is the cross alone that reveals what it means for the Son of God to sink to the bestial floor. Incarnate love sinks on the cross to the depths of suffering to which every victim has been thrust down, to bring the possibility of new life to those who have been nailed to all the thousand kinds of crosses. Incarnate love sinks even further into the state of the bestial and degraded, being crucified as a criminal and plunged into the godforsakenness of the guilty. "He descended into hell." The uncontrollable mystery makes his way down through the grave to the bestial floor of the alienated, guilty dead to bring them the good news that God is holding out a hand to raise them up into the light.

No one and no thing is outside the range of the new life that is the passionate, re-creative love of a suffering God. The whole gospel is present in all its fullness in each of its parts. The Epiphany at the manger opens the whole mystery to us. We need another year of grace to take it in. In fact, we will need all eternity.

Notes
1. W. B. Yeats, *Collected Poems* (New York: Macmillan, 1956), 124.
2. "Hymn XXXII," *Christopher Smart: Selected Poems,* ed. Marcus Walsh (Manchester: Carcanet, 1979), 99.

The Original *Abba*

T he furious controversy over the results of the cleaning of the Michelangelo frescos in the Sistine Chapel was wholly predictable. Quite apart from arguments about the techniques used, it was a shock to realize that the venerable patina everyone took for granted was nothing but muck and glue. The colors assault us now as impossibly sensuous and riotous. Robbed of their smoky veil, they seem blatantly new and we can't quite get rid of a feeling that some sort of sacrilege has been committed.

The art of restoring paintings seems to me to tell us something about the particular vocation of Anglican spirituality and theology at its best. Much that comes to us from the tradition is obscured under thick layers of overpainting and retouching. Original visions have been blotted out by layers of varnish. Great images of the divine have been turned into feeble holy pictures darkened by incense. If the tendency of Protestantism is to banish them to the attic, the Anglican approach is to uncover what lies under the familiar surface so that the original vision can reemerge in colors that may at first shock us. We are likely to upset those who have become devoted to the traditional appearance.

Few saints have been more affected by overpainting than St. Joseph. It happened to him very early as the apocryphal gospels encrusted the traditions about the nativity with groundless legends whose hidden purpose was to intensify the value of Mary's virginity. Therefore Joseph was transmogrified into an old gentleman who was suitable as a protector for a Mary who vowed herself to virginity from girlhood. In circles becoming ever more obsessed with virginity—a phenomenon that fascinated and scandalized pagans as distinctively Christian—it was held that Mary remained a virgin before, during, and after giving birth. No matter if this involved a disastrous compromising of the humanity of Jesus, who was proclaimed to have passed through her hymen like light through glass.

Apart from appearances as a bent-over figure in the corner of icons of the nativity, Joseph faded into obscurity. Where were the churches dedicated to him? Why so few hymns and works of art, or prayers? Naturally he is featured in medieval miracle plays of the nativity, but we cannot fail to notice that he has been made to resemble a stock figure of vulgar storytelling—the elderly cuckold!

In the west Joseph emerged from long obscurity into prominence at a particular juncture in the development of the western mentality. For two thousand years the word *familia*, family, had meant an entire household, including slaves, retainers, servants, and so on. It was perfectly natural to refer to a vast monastery as a family. In the late middle ages, however, a sense of individual self-awareness suddenly intensified and soon the word "family" was taken to refer only to parents and their children, a tight inner nexus of relationship. Father, mother, brothers, sisters round a single hearth. Fathers took on a new awareness of their role, and so there arose a powerful focus for devotion—the cult of the Holy Family. Here was the nuclear family in its essentials: mother, father, and child. Joseph was the new-found role model for fathers, the subject of reflection and prayer. A cult of the Holy Child developed and we are all familiar with the paintings and images that proliferated then.

Thanks to the doctrine of the perpetual virginity of Mary, this was a family from which sex had been banished. The role model for fathers of families was Mary's "spouse most chaste." At Christmas our tasteful greeting cards reproducing old masters serve up dozens of versions of this gentle, middle-aged man, wistful and emasculated. Thus the old Christian ambivalence about the goodness of sex was reinforced and the church made sure that virtually every model held up to men for emulation was sexless.

So what happens when we take our bottle of solvent and wipe away these layers of overpainting? The fresh, original colors of Scripture shine out. "When Joseph woke from sleep, he did as the angel of the Lord commanded him: he took Mary as his wife, but had no marital relations with her until she had borne a son; and he named him Jesus." For centuries Catholic exegetes had to obscure this text with a fog of grammatical prevarication to try to make it compatible with the dogma of the perpetual virginity of Mary, but we can accept the plain meaning of the words. After the birth of Jesus, Mary and Joseph entered into the fullness of the union they had longed for. "For this reason a man shall leave his father and his mother and be joined to his wife and the two shall become one flesh." The scriptures refer again and again to Jesus' brothers and sisters. We can wipe away the tortuous claims that they "must have been" children by a previous marriage of Joseph, or "must have been" cousins. On the contrary, the scriptures give no hint of the faintest incompatibility between Mary's virginal conception of Jesus and her subsequent bearing of other children to Joseph.

The tradition pictured the Holy Family as two parents who kept apart, and a solitary child. We all know families like that, but the vision based on Scripture is of a large family of boys and girls, Jesus being the eldest brother, with parents who slept together. Gone is the musty idea of Joseph as an old man. We can assume that by the time Jesus was baptized Joseph had died; by then he would have been over fifty. The graveyard at Nazareth would have been full of men who had died in their forties.

If we allow Joseph to regain his youth, his manhood, and his fatherhood in our imaginations, we can find that our devotion to him is deepened, not diminished. It was no emasculated wraith who, with Mary, evoked through love and touch the personhood of Jesus. Before Jesus learned to call God our Creator *Abba,* father, he called Joseph *Abba.* Joseph was the man who gave Jesus the sense that fatherhood was a glorious reality that imaged the infinite tenderness and strength of God.

What kind of man was this, whose own vitality and love gave to Jesus in his years as baby and boy that foundation of confidence on which would rest his absolute trust in the protective and enabling love of God? The kind of man who is entitled to our awestruck admiration and devotion, just as Mary is. We have a thousand images of Mary with Jesus at her breast, and we can never tire of saturating ourselves with their mystery and power. But the baby Jesus did not become the man Jesus by only being at the breast of Mary. The boy Jesus became the man Jesus by also being in the arms of a father.

In my imagination I can see the icon of Joseph I would like. It comes to me sometimes at the *sursum corda* of the eucharist: "Lift up your hearts!" Deep down these words touch a chord of memory we have of being lifted up as children. Again and again fathers reach down to take hold of their children under the armpits and swoop them into the air. Wasn't it bliss to soar upwards until our father's arms were stretched up high, to look down into a bright, upturned face from that fantastic height, and then to be clasped to a strong chest, allowed to merge for a moment with its magnificent strength?

"Lift up your hearts!" the celebrant cries at the eucharist, and once again I am invited to soar up and merge with the strength and vitality of an infinitely tender and life-giving God. Sometimes the thought of Joseph comes to me then, doing this for Jesus. Lifting him up, holding him up, looking up at him with wonder against the bright sky, while he cried laughingly, *"Abba,* Father." This is how Jesus learnt love, just as he did through the face, the breasts, and the arms of Mary.

Never has there been any time in history which more called for devotion to the Holy Family and meditation on what it is to communicate life through parenthood. Maybe the restorer's solvents and rags have helped us to see more of the original picture we are called to contemplate.

Desire

Who Do You Say That I Am?

The Twelfth Sunday after Pentecost,
at the Church of St. Michael and St. George, St. Louis

B eneath the surface of what we say to one another there is a great mass of what goes unsaid, of what we fail to say or are afraid to say. Understandably, we don't often talk about the things we don't say and why we don't say them, but we should. What goes unsaid has enormous power. An iceberg moves not because the wind blows upon its surface, but because its vast bulk hidden beneath the water is moved by the currents in the depths.

Sadly, many of us do not realize the power of the unsaid until a loved one dies without warning. Suddenly there is an agonizing awareness of things we wanted to say, but the chance has passed and it is too late now. We experience terrible regret about all the things we left unsaid, cursing ourselves for the lethargy or procrastination that held us back while the loved one was alive. Those who minister to the bereaved constantly hear: "You know, I'd gotten out of the habit of saying I loved her. I was never very demonstrative; I just took it for granted that she knew I did. If only I'd told her before her operation how much she meant to me! How could I have been so mean, so stupid?"…"You know, I'd been thinking for months that it was time to phone my dad and arrange to go home so we could be reconciled. I'd gotten over my bitterness. It was time to forgive. But I didn't do it. Now he is dead and our last words were the angry ones we threw at each other two years ago. Why didn't I tell him I wanted to be reconciled? Why didn't I say what I felt?"

For some of us guilt is the major component of the pain of bereavement. Death has exposed our tendency to take others for granted, our lack of generosity in failing to express our appreciation. In life we used the excuse that others could tell how we felt; in death that excuse is unmasked as a shabby lie used to cover our parsimony. We left the people we love to assume that we appreciated them instead of actually giving them our appreciation regularly, in simple words.

It is not only the bereaved who experience the enormous negative power of the unspoken. It is typical of families and groups to conspire together to banish into the realm of the unspeakable some truth they feel is too awful to accept. So we get the fantastic versatility of alcoholic households in not referring in any way to what is glaringly obvious—the devastating addiction of one of its members, the drinking problem that is the source of their daily misery. It is amazing what people will live with as long as no one tells the truth.

In the same way, gay adults have the common experience of being welcome at their parents home, even with their companions, on the condition that complete silence is maintained on the subject of homosexuality. If anyone actually dares to state the obvious, a volcanic eruption of rage may lead to banishment and estrangement. Why did he or she have to spoil the game by bringing the truth out of the safe realm of the unspoken?

We leave important truths locked up in the realm of the unspoken out of inertia and out of fear of the sanctions individuals and groups impose against those who break a conspiracy of silence. But we also fail to say certain things because we are afraid of ourselves rather than of others—afraid to commit ourselves. As long as something is left unsaid we can remain undecided, toy with various options, remain safe and concealed, free to backtrack. But when we let something out of the realm of the unspoken we are identifying ourselves, committing ourselves with all the attendant risks. Perhaps you have friends who have told you what it felt like to stand up in their first AA meeting and say "I am Joseph, I am an alcoholic." Or maybe you can remember what it was like to say "I love you" for the first time. As long as love is unspoken, only hinted at in romantic banter and flirting, then you can go back on it. But when you take your life into your hands and say "I love you," then suddenly love is present in all its awesome power.

It is not only fear of commitment that makes us leave unsaid so much that cries out to be said; it is also fear of change. When we say things with words, we change situations. We expose ourselves to contradiction and struggle as others deal with what we have committed ourselves to. Who knows where that will lead?

Unless we reckon with the presence and power of the unspoken, we cannot enter into today's gospel or experience what Jesus is doing with his disciples. They have gone into pagan territory. Caesarea Philippi was a pagan spa, with a shrine to the god Pan set in the red cliffs where the water flows out. Jesus has decided that the time is ripe for them to talk about what they think of him. So far it has all been left safely unspoken. He gives them an easy way in by asking them what people in general are saying about him. "Who do they say that the Son of Man is?" The disciples don't mind answering that. "Oh, they think you are pretty spooky; they think that the spirit of dead John the Baptist has entered into you, or one of the prophets of old."

"But who do YOU say that I am?" We can feel the awkward silence that follows. Until now the disciples could maintain a "wait and see" attitude, could hedge their bets. Now Jesus is asking all of them, one by one, to look him in the eyes and say what he means to them. No one says a thing—until Peter, the most impetuous, takes courage and dares to say that Jesus, the carpenter from Nazareth, is the Christ, the Son of the Living God. Suddenly the awful truth has been named, things can never be the same again, and Jesus blesses Peter for trusting and declaring the truth God has revealed to him.

This incident throws a flood of light on the business of praying. What is prayer? Prayer is giving Christ the chance to look me in the eye and ask me, "But who do *you* say that I am?" In prayer we say to God, to Christ, who he is for us. If you are one of those churchgoers who doesn't pray except for a moment or two in the pew, or at odd moments when the mood arises or when you need something, you will know how nice and safe it is never to tell Christ who he is for you. It can remain unexpressed, unspoken, vague, obscure. Oh, you can recite the creed in church and sing a few hymns, but that is not the same as owning up to your own real feelings and attitudes and beliefs.

"What is the point of it?" those who don't pray retort. "Why bother to tell Christ what he must already know? Isn't he supposed to know everything?" The objection is based on a complete misunderstanding. The purpose of expressing our own feelings and attitudes and desires and beliefs and doubts and fears to God is not to convey information, but to bring them out of the safe realm of the unspoken and deal with them in the open. The fact is that we don't *know* what we really feel about Christ, about his presence or his seeming absence, his power in our lives or his seeming impotence. We don't know how much we love him, we don't know we are angry and disappointed with him until we bring these things out of obscurity. The Risen Christ asks us, "Who do you say that I am?" not to seek information but to bring the truth out of our hearts.

Expressing is giving. When I say to someone I love, "You mean everything to me," I am not merely informing that person, I am loving him with words. Christ asks us to say who he is for us to encourage us to give voice to our love for him.

We don't pray because to face what is real between God and ourselves is demanding. How hard it is to bring out the truth from the closet of the unspoken, the unsaid! And yet how wonderful to begin to get the hang of telling the truth to Christ, coming out with what is really going on between us. "Christ, you scare the hell out of me because I think of you as one who wants to change my life, and I don't want to change." "Christ, I need your companionship; I am married, I have kids, I have a great job, but I feel lonely and it terrifies me."

If we can truly hear Christ speaking to us through today's gospel, we will be encouraged to experiment in this struggle to express our real self to him. If you tend to limit your conversation with God to a few set prayers now and then, you might deliberately choose this coming week to sit somewhere private where no one can disturb you for about fifteen minutes. Listen to Christ's question, "Who do *you* say that I am?" Let some answers emerge in your heart. Express those answers to him and don't convert them into pious language or censor your feelings. Let them out.

Or you could set aside a time to do nothing for ten minutes except repeat, "God, I love you." You may feel reluctant, embarrassed. You may tell yourself you don't, so you have no right to say it. But just say it. The heart of our religion is to love God with all our mind, with all our heart, with all our soul, and with all our strength. So why do we leave our love—the love we want to have, or we wouldn't be Christians—unsaid? Prayer like this gives voice to that part of ourselves we so often ruthlessly silence and repress, that part of ourselves that has faith, love, and hope.

Singing with
the Angels

Summer, at the monastery

I t is remarkable that there are only a few more than four
hundred plots in all the world's folk tales. The bag of tricks
that is the human psyche holds a finite number of tricks, and
fairy tales use them all. Think how revealing is that wonderful
moment in _Snow White_ when the Queen interrogates her mirror:

> "Mirror, mirror on the wall,
>   who is the fairest of them all?"
> "Thou wert fairest once, O Queen.
>   Snow White is fairest now, I ween."

I was feeling a bit sympathetic with the Queen yesterday, on
my forty-fifth birthday. We want the mirror to reassure us that
things are still the same—how rude of it to insist on giving us
the unwelcome message, "That was then, this is now." And
how much we want our sense of superiority to others to be mirrored back at us. It pains our vanity to be told that someone
else surpasses us in the very virtues we want to monopolize.

Reading between the lines of the sayings of the desert fathers, it appears that from the very beginning they were susceptible to the illusion that monks were superior in prayer to

ordinary folk. There are telling stories of how they were briskly disillusioned, just like the Queen in Snow White. No doubt St. Anthony of Egypt was in a "mirror, mirror on the wall" mood when it was revealed to him in his prayer "that there was one who was his equal in the city. He was a doctor by profession, and whatever he had beyond his needs he gave to the poor, and every day he sang Holy, Holy, Holy with the angels."

In this story every word counts. Anthony is coolly told that the contemplative goal of the desert hermit can be attained in the bustle of a great port city. The radical poverty of the monk is more than matched by the generosity of a layman who gives everything away beyond what he needs. What is more, the fundamental aim of monastic prayer, which is continuous, moment-by-moment attention to the mystery of God, can be achieved by a busy professional seeing patients from morning till night. Like the angels in the vision of Isaiah, the doctor never ceases from the praise that cries, "Holy, Holy, Holy is the Lord of hosts, the whole earth is full of his glory."

Stories like this crop up throughout the entire body of monastic literature, and monks told them against themselves, puncturing their own fantasies of superiority. But when you give them some thought, their stories are equally capable of giving a jolt to layfolk. It is a convenient illusion for laypeople to feel that they are exempt from the call of continuous prayer because that is reserved for monastics. We are not sure we like the physician of Alexandria—what is all this about continuous prayer? How did he manage this constant awareness of God while elbowing his way through the docks to get to plague-infested slums or coping with the screams of sick children in his surgery?

If we are honest we have to admit that we are very skeptical about the desirability of continuous prayer. It is not something we really want to believe is possible; it suits us to think of God as someone we can visit from time to time, like a loving grandparent or a consoling friend. But in fact it is also nice to get away from someone we love, someone who does us good.

Many of us know the guilty pleasure of *not* being with the one you love. It's a bit of a relief, isn't it? We don't want them around all the time. For most of us the idea of always being in God's company is quite horrifying, like one of those prison cells in which they leave the light on all the time.

So people like the physician of Alexandria reveal to us the extent of our mistrust of God, and our need to feel out of God's presence a good deal of the time. We think they must have some secret we can't seem to get at because continuous prayer seems like incessantly having to do two things at once. It suggests a weird, split consciousness in which this doctor is lancing boils and mixing ointments "on automatic pilot" while his mind is miles away singing with the angels. We have a sneaking suspicion that we might see his lips move in prayer and his eyes show a faraway look as he moves toward us with his lancet; we make a mental note to check whether our health plan will let us change doctors.

All of us have made ambitious attempts to pray continuously. We try to sustain and prolong prayers of petition, intercession, and devotion as we go about our business. We practice the Jesus prayer. Then suddenly we collide into another shopper in the department store who chews us out, or we nearly step under a bus. The price we paid for our devotion was to lose awareness of our surroundings. It's a bit dangerous and a bit unreal. Far safer to limit ourselves to visiting with God now and then.

Yet those who actually practice continuous prayer tell us it does *not* lead to divided consciousness; in fact, they assure us that prayer is how we are healed from it. The physician of Alexandria was not tuning out his patients' lives, for the cryptic phrase "singing with the angels" is meant to remind us of Jesus' saying that the angels "continually see the face of my Father in heaven." We are being told that the physician had come to the point of knowing himself to be in the presence of God in everything and everywhere. His response to that presence was a continuous leaning into it like the angels, a leaning toward the face of God and a moment-by-moment breathing of worship, like the simple angelic song of "Holy, Holy, Holy."

So these men and women of continuous prayer encounter a God who can be recognized and loved throughout the day, and yet this worship does not take our attention away from the people and events with which we have to do, but actually heightens it. As Alan Watts wrote, mystical awareness of God does not drive away other experiences and states of mind: "There is no conflict between experiencing the Now and the things that happen in the Now."

For someone like myself, who is as afflicted by chronic mental preoccupation as anyone, this image has been a talisman and an Ariadne's thread as I try to make my way in the hope of a more constant openness to God moment by moment. There are many situations in which I have made no headway at all, but for many years I have had use of the key to a deep awareness of God in public places, among crowds. Most of us have a sense of God in places of great natural beauty, but the test of the practice of the presence of God lies in the settings that seem the most barren, anonymous, and profane—the malls, the airports, the fast-food restaurants, the subway stations, the crowds in the street. I have to admit to you that these are the very situations in which God has for a long time most pressed upon my heart.

We only have to turn off our Walkmans, put our magazines away, surrender our anxieties, and become aware of where we are. We only have to say to ourselves the great words of truth, *here* and *now*. Take in what is happening in the here and now. It is a crowded New York subway, infernally hot, with a sense of vague menace and anxiety in the air. It is a coffee shop—someone in the corner is smoking a Gitane cigarette. And the *now* in which these people are and these things are happening is God who holds us all in life. The *here* and the *now* is God, who gives birth to it all. The *here* and the *now* is Jesus, God's offspring made flesh, who ascended above the heavens that he might fill all things, including this subway station and this coffee shop and all the people in it with me. The *here* and the *now* is the Spirit, the one breath we are all breathing.

Is it so hard to sing along with the angels in some quiet place inside, "Holy, Holy, Holy"? It's not so hard. You can do it while feeling glad—in a mood of exultation, when you wonder how it is that God stays just under the surface of life, like a whale not coming up to breathe, just beneath the deck of everyday consciousness. You can do it while feeling sad—sad at the way we wreck life and sad at the pain and distraction on the perspiring faces of those in the subway car. You can do it while feeling mad—mad at frustrations and disappointments but still leaning toward the Face in the coffee shop, still singing along with the angels. And you can do it while being bad—still sensing God even when insisting on your own way, recognizing even then that the sins of the world do not take away the Lamb of God. It's the other way around.

Questioning
Our Desires

Lent, at the Church of the Holy Cross, Troy, New York

O ne of the characters in Dorothy L. Sayers's novel *Gaudy Night* recalls at one point "the extempore prayer of a well meaning but incoherent curate... 'Lord, teach us to take our hearts and look them in the face, however difficult it may be.'" This odd but profound prayer tells us what Lent should be all about, because one of the gifts of the Spirit is the ability to decipher the language of our desires and to come to understand their deep meanings.

One of the basic features of the life of faith is that it does not take things at their face value or judge by mere appearances. For the believer things are seldom what they seem. In fact, the life of faith has much in common with the enterprise of science. Both of them stand in contrast to the conventional, secular mind that takes appearances literally and straightforwardly, asking no further questions once something has been taken in at first glance. The profane mind reacts to immediate appearances and asks no further questions; the religious mind keeps on asking questions in search of the deepest meanings behind all appearances. On this all the world's scriptures agree, from the ancient Upanishads, which tell us "the gods hate the obvious and love the obscure," to our own New Testament, in which Paul's words to the Corinthians are typical:

> Those who are unspiritual do not receive the gifts of God's Spirit, for they are foolishness to them, and they are unable to understand them because they are spiritually discerned. (1 Cor. 2:14)

That the ways of God and the truth of life are not obvious is focused for us, of course, in the cross. It is not obvious, to say the least, that the execution of a Galilean workman was the supreme act of God's love for us.

The difference between the two attitudes I am contrasting is far-reaching and leads to very different patterns of behavior. Typically, the literal-minded types will take their own desires at their face value; the constant waves of emotion and impulse and desire do not lead them to further questions, but are taken as cues for immediate action. In the worst cases these people live life according to the motto "I want what I want when I want it." We know people like this; some of us may even have to live and work with them. Perhaps a large number keep on trying to satisfy the ceaseless flow of desires but are frustrated by the fact that satisfaction does not assuage desire. My favorite expression of this prevalent experience is from Saul Bellow's novel *Henderson the Rain King:*

> Now I have already mentioned that there was a disturbance in my heart, a voice that spoke there and said, *I want, I want, I want!* It happened every afternoon and when I tried to suppress it it got even stronger. It only said one thing, *I want, I want, I want.*
>
> And I would ask, "What do you want?" But this is all it would ever tell me. It never said a thing except *I want, I want, I want!* At times I would treat it like an ailing child whom you offer rhymes or candy. I would walk it, I would trot it. I would sing to it or read to it. No use. I would change into overalls

and go up on the ladder and spackle cracks in the ceiling: I would chop wood, go out and drive a tractor, work in the barn among the pigs. No, No!

Through fights and drunkenness and labor it went right on, in the country, in the city. No purchase however expensive would lessen it. Then I would say, "Come on, tell me. What's the complaint, is it Lily herself? Do you want some nasty whore? It has to be some lust?" But this was no better a guess than the others. The demand came louder, *I want, I want, I want, I want, I want, I want!* And I would cry, begging at last, "Oh, tell me then. Tell me what you want!"[1]

This racy passage, so funny and yet so full of pathos, expresses the bafflement of many contemporaries who find that the manifold satisfactions at hand in our culture do not assuage the maddening, insistent hunger of the heart.

Another strategy consists of anesthetizing desire instead of attempting to satisfy it. One can use business, or alcohol, or lulling domestic routine to blot desires out and become a person who has given up wanting or searching or yearning for anything whatever—other than the same again, please.

It is conversion that gradually leads us into the understanding of desire, the ability to decipher the language of passions, and slowly teaches us to let the energy of our desiring lead us home to God. At the heart of conversion is the insight expressed in the prayer of St. Augustine, "Our heart is restless until it finds its rest in thee." The desires of the restless human heart are real and significant and to be reckoned with, but their deepest meaning is to draw us to wanting, needing, and loving God.

Today's gospel tells us of a crucial experience of Jesus in deciphering his own desires. In the wilderness Jesus was tested as to his willingness to go on questioning his desires until he reached the point of discovering that he really desired God and God's ways. The Holy Spirit left nothing to chance, inciting Jesus to get away from everything and everybody in order to hear the voices of desire within himself. What went on is expressed in the form of a dramatic dialogue with Satan, the spiritual tester of human flaws and weak points.

Jesus wants food. Out there, miles from anywhere, the only way of getting something to eat is to force a miracle. Jesus wants food, but does he want to force God's hand with a miracle just to fill his belly? No, he doesn't want that. He wants much more to carry on listening to what God is saying to him as he fasts. That is what he truly desires.

Then Jesus feels the intense urgency of making an impact on the world at large. Surely he wants to secure that massive impact by allying himself with the powers that be, by going political? No, Jesus really desires to focus unswervingly on God his Father and to owe him absolute loyalty, even if that means having no guarantees of success in the world. That is what he really wants.

Then Jesus wants to bring his message to the people with the dramatic force of a lightning flash. Does he want to go straight to the temple, the spiritual powerhouse and national center, and burst onto the scene with a terrific miraculous impact? Jesus questions his desire and goes on to discover that what in fact he desires is to be obedient to God, who won't take shortcuts and won't be manipulated, the God who works slowly and in secret through changed and healed lives. Jesus desires to trust God rather than set God up for a test.

The wilderness of Judea is still dotted with remote monasteries; some of them have been going for 1500 years. The monks saw their desert monasteries as laboratories for testing the meaning of the heart's desires. We don't go literally into a wilderness, but Lent is our desert time as we do the same research into our own lives. True self-examination is the quest to find God through our desires.

So, for example, we pay attention to our sexual desires, which are incredibly varied, insistent, and pervasive. If we were literalists we would take them at face value as purely biological urges or appetites to be met in the forms that our fantasies dictate. Instead, we look into our hearts and attend to the need for intimacy, which is the deeper meaning of our desires. We discern how to bring our need into relationship with the needs of others so that there can be mutual fulfillment. We try to be realistic, knowing that much of our sexual need won't find literal satisfaction.

But the quest for meaning doesn't stop there. Even when people find full satisfaction of their needs for intimacy in marriage, partnership, friendship, and family, there is still a depth of craving in the heart. Our sexuality is the clue to a deep, basic need to be desirable and to desire and a profound urge toward ecstasy and bliss. And this clue has been planted in the heart by God, who is love. If we will let them, our desires tell us that we long to be found lovable and desirable by God and that we long to give ourselves up to God's loveliness and glory and tenderness. Whether we find disappointment or fulfillment in our search for intimacy, it is the key to a new life to discover that we are made to be in love with God.

One of the reasons why so many Christians don't know that loving God is a matter of intimacy and passion and tenderness, not mere obedience and service, is that they have not looked their hearts in the face and seen there a deep, deep longing for unconditional love. So if we keep on paying attention to our sexuality and questioning our desires, we come to know ourselves as men and women of desire who are not ashamed to bring to God in prayer our passionate need to be desired and loved.

Sexual desire is just one example. In every kind of desire there is an immense amount that the Spirit can teach us. We find ourselves full of anxious desires to keep working and working, to please everyone around whatever it costs. What is the desire behind the desires? It seems that we desire approval. Perhaps others will esteem us if we show ourselves so conscientious and obliging. And what is the desire even deeper than that desire? We find that underneath we crave to be cherished for exactly who we are, regardless of our labors.

Through the questions we ask of our desires, the Spirit leads us back to our deep woundedness, a basic doubt about our own value. Our overwork can satisfy the surface desires but can do nothing to heal the basic wound from which the drivenness comes.

Here the Spirit has taken us to the level of basic healing of our souls, the level of redemption. Only God, who made us, who knows us through and through, who has searched us out in Jesus and is utterly for us and with us, only God is able to heal that wound of self-doubt from which so much of our un-trusting and compulsive behavior springs. So we learn not merely to pray about the symptoms but to pray about the cause, asking Jesus to fill that void inside with this assurance of his love for us. The satisfaction of being approved of is a substitute for the real thing, this sense of being real and valu-able and honored because Christ is in us and we are in him. The more we seek the real thing in prayer, the less we find we need to rely on substitutes.

It is a travesty of Christian spirituality to imagine that the ba-sic spiritual struggle is fighting to smother and suppress our de-sires. This movement of growth is in fact learning to understand their real meaning. Awareness of all our chaotic feelings keeps us humble and aware. In humility we grow to recognize very deep needs which only God can satisfy. We can tolerate the fact that our lovers and neighbors aren't supposed to satisfy desires that only God can fulfill. We learn to turn those deep needs toward God and become better at asking, knocking, asking, and thirsting after him. In learning to desire, we come to know that God desires us.

Notes
1. Saul Bellow, *Henderson the Rain King* (New York: Penguin, 1976), 24.

Let Your "No" Be No

Advent, at the monastery

"Let your 'Yes' be yes and your 'No' be no," urged St. James, quoting words of Jesus that Matthew included in the Sermon on the Mount. They spring from Jesus' own candor and directness and invite us to practice a seamless honesty like his that never needs reinforcing with oaths. But what strikes me now is that they assume that the word "no" is going to be continually on the lips of the disciples. Apparently "no" is not a bad word. Jesus implies that "no" can be just as holy as "yes." Refusal as well as denial has its part to play in life and we are invited to say "no" out of freedom and confidence. We are invited to learn how to say "no" with faith.

Yet that is exactly what a great number of us find horribly difficult. Saying "no" strikes me as one of the chief places of bad faith in many of our lives, a place of insecurity and guilt. Just listen to the language we use in talking about how busy we are: "Oh, the fall has been so busy....The weeks before Christmas our home is going to be a zoo....I haven't stopped for weeks...." We fall into a common rhetoric of overextension, making rueful inventories of our crowding obligations and dense schedules.

Our ruefulness is of dubious sincerity. On the one hand we in this community feel like braining people when they say, "Oh, I know you are all so very, very busy, but...." Yet we can never find it in ourselves to say, "No, I'm not busy, I keep things simple and make sure some time is free." That might open us to the accusation of laziness. The same ambivalence about chronic overcrowding of life is present in most of the stories we hear from the people we see in spiritual direction, the same curious blend of shame and pride in the fact that our boat has so many passengers and so much cargo that it only just stays afloat.

We could of course handle this topic on the merely human level by talking about the "pace of life" and all that. We could think managerially about how we use our time. Or therapeutically, by asking how we can find time to "nurture ourselves," as the current jargon blithely puts it. Or, as Christians, we could look at it in the light of the incarnation of the Life and Word of God in Jesus. If we do, maybe we shall find that our inability to say "no," our confusion about limitations, is deeply embedded in our fallenness. Maybe we need to be saved here with a healing that reaches pretty deep down.

In our inability to say "no," our tendency to consent to excessive invitations and demands, our readiness to mask our disagreement with the pleasing word "yes," we will almost certainly be right in suspecting the presence of deep fear. For many it is the fear of alienating others and being rejected on account of our refusal. We might smile at the pathetic letters from teenagers in the advice columns of magazines, describing how they gave in to the sexual demands of their partners because they were afraid of being dropped. The same dynamic is present in our own relationships, however, more than we would like to admit. If we were secure in our sense of lovableness and could act out of this source of trust, we could let our "no" be no. But not many of us are, so we try to maintain our relationships with the yeses of bad faith.

The second fear is that of condemnation. I dread the accusation of selfishness and idleness and lack of response when someone wants to see me and I am already committed. But to say "no" is too frightening, so I start to perform an operation on my datebook that has all the grace and integrity of one of

Cinderella's ugly sisters trying to get her foot into the glass slipper. I think of a friend who is a dedicated peace activist and who has become humorless, gray, and strung-out; behind her liberal spirituality lurks a fear of the condemnation of God not all that different from the fear embedded in old-time hellfire religion. We know all the texts about going the second mile and "When you have done all that you were ordered to do, say, 'We are worthless slaves; we have only done what we ought to have done!'" It doesn't take much to make us hear the gospel as a taskmaster's sentence to unlimited obligation and toil.

Then there is another level of dread. "Yes" is the word of actualization by which we open ourselves to yet another experience, to a new relationship, sensation, acquisition, to new memories. "No" is the word of renunciation; it relinquishes opportunity and experimentation; it passes things up. Our trouble with "no" will usually reveal our trouble with limitation itself, with finitude, boundaries, a short span and restricted space, and with the final limit of our death. Often we say "yes" because "no" reminds us of death, of not having, of not feeling, of not being. Not long ago I saw an advertisement for some firm that offers financial services that proclaimed, "No boundaries!" It sounds brave, and yet if you mull it over it begins to sound like a curse.

Recently some words from the first letter of John have seemed to me the very definition of the gospel:

> There is no fear in love, but perfect love casts out fear; for fear has to do with punishment, and whoever fears has not reached perfection in love. We love because he first loved us. (1 John 4:18-19)

Perfect love casts out fear. That is what we celebrate in Advent, the coming into our lives of a love that is more powerful than our chronic, defensive fear.

I want to invite you to meditate on this coming with the help of two great words derived from the scriptures, fullness and self-emptying. The scriptures say of Jesus that "in him all the fullness of God was pleased to dwell" (Col. 1:19). Fullness is unqualified relatedness to God, giving freedom to spend oneself. It expresses the gift of inner centeredness and substance and worth that liberates us from futile grasping. But that fullness is not individual self-realization, maximum wealth of experience. The life of the one who was filled with all the fullness of God was a limited life, confined to the little towns of Israel, cut short when his mission was rejected and he was executed as a rebel and blasphemer. This fullness of life is intimately bound up with self-emptying, which reconciles us with our finiteness, enables us to embrace limitation, gives us the freedom to submit to the vanishing point of death out of trust in God.

Many of us keep on saying "yes" when "no" is really called for because we are bargaining for affirmation. We will be loved if we say "yes." But suppose we discovered that the void of unlovableness that drives us to the bargaining table is itself an illusion?

This is conversion—the discovery that our worthlessness is an illusion. The mystery of faith is that we need not patch together a self or an identity. That self we seek, that center, that identity, is there already because it is given. It is Christ. Christ is the self we were trying to find. Christ is our life. Repentance comes when the reality of that sinks in, when it begins to dawn on me that Christ dwells in my heart through faith. This strange little life of mine is being filled with all the fullness of God. Then I can start letting my "no" be no without fear of falling to pieces or ruining my relationships. Perfect love, the unconditional love that is Christ living in me, casts out fear.

It is out of this fullness that we can let our lives take the shape of his "who, though he was in the form of God, did not regard equality with God as something to be exploited, but emptied himself, taking the form of a slave" (Phil. 2:5-6). In Advent we allow the incarnation to move us again as a mystery of God's choice to embrace the limitations of human life. We place ourselves ready to find the manger and the swaddling clothes wringing our hearts with a sense of littleness and fragility and restriction, and it is as if we too are invited to the same choice. I can either live in the endless striving to extend my life through endless pursuit of fulfillment—or I can choose to be *this* person, to have *this* life, here, bounded, precarious, constrained by suffering and the vanishing point of death.

I am free to say "no" without resentment and regrets because I have chosen to be incarnate in my own body, in this place and this time, and have allowed its particularities, its gifts and griefs, to be my "form of a slave." I can let my "no" be no with faith because it flows from the "yes" of incarnation.

Conversion

The Peril of
the Eucharist

L et us admit the power eucharistic hospitality has in our
lives. Here we all are, some friends, some strangers, all of
us in a sense strangers with our private lives, hopes, and fears.
Yet here we come round an altar and all receive an identical
welcome, the same invitation—Come! eat! drink! praise!—the
same sense of family. Not to be sneezed at in a fragmented
and incoherent society like ours, this well-being of belonging,
this free assurance of identity with others. Our church has
done its utmost lately to give the liturgy a corporate pattern
and to make celebrations of the eucharist more frequent, em-
phasizing the open fellowship of our altars with the offer of
communion to the baptized of all churches.

But charm is dangerous. There can arise a false sense of security in eucharistic participation that makes us deaf to the
hard questions the church has to put to us about the integrity
of our communion. In accepting so blithely the invitation to
the eucharist, are you being dishonest, or might you be delud-
ing yourself about what is going on and blinding yourself to
the consequences that follow?

Modern ministers hesitate to appear to be sending mixed
signals by warning people to think long and hard about com-

ing to communion, so it is a good thing that Paul in his vigorous and rigorous way had no such hesitations. It is time to recall his trenchant response to the cliquish pot-luck supper into which the eucharist at Corinth had degenerated. He warns these Christians:

> Whoever, therefore, eats the bread or drinks the cup of the Lord in an unworthy manner will be answerable for the body and blood of the Lord. Examine yourselves, and only then eat of the bread and drink of the cup. For all who eat and drink without discerning the body, eat and drink judgment against themselves. For this reason many of you are weak and ill, and some have died. But if we judged ourselves, we would not be judged. (1 Cor. 11:27-31)

Some of these words are extremely offensive to our ears. Paul actually attributes the sickness and death of some members to the nonchalance with which they had been taking communion. We recoil from the hypothesis that the Lord's Supper can be lethal if handled heedlessly. Well, let us make allowances, if we like, for Paul's intensely realistic way of viewing things. What we must *not* do is attempt to reduce the seriousness with which the eucharist is taken as the scene of judgment. The Lord's Supper is a glorious and a perilous happening. If we approach it without the authentic faith, recognition, and discernment that it calls for, then our participation hardens and coarsens us; the act confirms and intensifies our insensitivity and lack of integrity.

The words "For all who eat and drink without discerning the body, eat and drink judgment against themselves" are part of the very earliest account of the eucharist. The gospel narratives of the Last Supper were written later. We cannot get behind this understanding of the sacrament to an imagined more primitive and milder attitude—nor will we get far turning the pages of the New Testament to find passages without this judgment theme. The discourse of Jesus at Capernaum in John's gospel about eating the flesh and drinking the blood of the Son of Man causes offense and division, leading at once to the theme of disbelief and betrayal:

> "But among you there are some who do not believe." For Jesus knew from the first who were the ones that did not believe, and who was the one that would betray him. (John 6:64)

When Paul hands over the tradition of the Lord's Supper, it begins, "On the night he was betrayed." In Luke's gospel there is an appalling juxtaposition of the word of blessing over the bread and cup, and the pronouncement of judgment on the betrayer:

> This cup that is poured out for you is the new covenant in my blood. But see, the one who betrays me is with me, and his hand is on the table. (Luke 22:20-21)

The earliest fragments of liturgy we possess also dramatically express the judgment theme. Paul ended his first letter to the Corinthians with a solemn liturgical verse of warning in his own handwriting:

> Let anyone be accursed who has no love for the Lord. *Maranatha!* Our Lord, come! The grace of the Lord Jesus be with you. (1 Cor. 16:22-23)

Liturgical material in the primitive text called the *Didache* (older than some books of the New Testament) fills this verse out: "If any be a sinner let him repent. If any be holy let him draw near, *Maranatha! Maranatha!* Let grace come and this age pass away!" The first full rites we possess do not waver from this theme. "Lord Holy Spirit, obtain for us this food of your holiness so that it may not turn to our judgment nor to our shame or our condemnation, but to the healing and consolation of our own spirit."

No wonder that the early church had a secret discipline that prevented pagans and even candidates for baptism from taking part in the eucharistic meal itself. Full initiation into a relationship of informed faith was necessary if the church was not to endanger people by bringing them prematurely into the perilous field of force that is communion in the body and blood of Christ.

The fact that our practice and mentality have altered so much makes it all the more important to keep hold of the truth in which these beliefs were rooted—the truth that if we deny Christ in some way and at the same time approach the eucharist, we are encountering the very One we are resisting. The real presence of Christ makes our denial into a direct refusal and betrayal and this rebounds upon us as judgment. The gifts bring with them the Giver. We cannot paralyze God's action by our lack of faith or love. We cannot by our lack of recognition turn the presence of Christ into absence.

The first kind of denial by which we risk judgment in the eucharist is denial of the resurrection and of the real presence, the failure to discern the risen body of the Lord through which we participate in the gifts. The core of the gospel is that our brother who gave his life for us on the cross has been, in a unique divine act of transformation, taken out of the grip of the disintegration and death that is our fate. Of this glorification the empty tomb and the appearances were the signs that tell us that now we are bound to hope. The route of despair has been closed off. The resurrection means that we cannot but live and hope for the redemption of all things. His resurrection is the rehearsal, the beginning, the anticipation of ours. Now, as we live in the crucifyingly obscure time between his resurrection and ours, Christ comes to us in the meal of the eucharist. In these signs the Risen Lord incorporates food into his spiritual body and as we feed upon them we are incorporated into his person in anticipation of the ultimate transformation that still awaits us.

Consequently, the church has to say to its friends who do not believe in the resurrection but still desire our fellowship, "Worship with us, study, serve alongside us, talk, pray with us for further light, but be truthful about where you are. Please do not take communion. Wait. These gifts must not meet agnosticism or denial in your heart. Without faith in the Risen One the heart has no choice but to demote these mysteries into mere tokens, to strip them of the meaning with which in the Great Thanksgiving they have been awesomely invested. An act of spiritual violence is going on here that we beg you not to commit and warn you not to risk."

The second type of denial is the one that directly stimulated Paul's response. The expression about not discerning the body is, I think, deliberately ambiguous. On the one hand it refers to the relegation of the eucharistic gifts to the level of mundane food; some of the Corinthians overate and some got drunk. But equally seriously, the ruin of the eucharist lay in the breaking up of the assembly along social and class lines and the failure to discern the church as the body of Christ.

We are warned therefore that a wholehearted commitment to the life and the unity of our particular congregation is essential to the integrity of our communion. I must ask myself, "Am I content, even proud, to live selfishly on the margin of, or even in contempt of, the church, the flesh and blood community? Am I refusing forgiveness to anyone, or not seeking it from someone? Is my heart hardened against any fellow communicant? Am I indifferent to the hunger and thirst of the millions even as I eat and drink the sacrament?" If the answer is yes, then perhaps I eat and drink judgment upon myself. Better to refrain, rethink, repent, and then return.

The third type of refusal is anything that implicitly denies that the bread and the cup proclaim the Lord's *death* until his coming again, anything that represses the awful truth that this is the body and blood of the Crucified One. In communion we take our lives in our hands and commit ourselves to dying, in and with Christ, to sin. This does not mean that only the sinless may take communion—that is absurd. But it does mean that communion involves our surrender to the forgiveness and the purgation of Christ's crucified love, or it is not communion at all. If we in any place in our lives deliberately withhold that surrender, and hold out against that dying to self the Crucified One asks of us as he offers us his love, then in our nonchalant communion we mock and deny him. We eat and drink judgment upon ourselves, and Incarnate Love is betrayed at this table as he was at the first in the upper room.

The Print of Otherness

Eastertide, at the monastery

"Well," I said to a lilac tree in a street on the west side of New York last week, "I won't be using the shepherd theme for my homily because I've never known any shepherds." "Oh, but you did know one once," replied the lilac tree, as the scent of its blossoms transported me in a moment to the spring of 1965.

We all know that growing up is a very uneven business. There are some weeks, even days—and certainly some nights—in which one does more growing up than in a whole previous year. In the spring I'm thinking of, I left an English boarding school in the shadow of a cathedral to work as a bricklayer for six months for the Taizé community in France.

Within a matter of hours the delicate structure of gentlemanly sensibilities inculcated by English education began to be undermined. After a few days there a group of Portuguese scouts visited the house where the building team lived, and I managed conversation quite well (I thought) in my halting and pedantic French. But at the end of the meal there was a sudden movement for which I was not prepared. The cloth was whisked from the table, guitars appeared from nowhere, and a wild, sensuous thrumming began to sound. Two of the Portuguese leapt onto the table and began to dance, their heels throbbing on the wood, gyrating and snapping their fingers as the guitars drummed and twanged. Dancing! On the table! I was speechless with horror and amazement. After a few minutes I staggered out into the square and sat under the lilac trees to recover.

It was then that the shepherd introduced himself to me, crushing my hand in an iron grip, his expression fiercely interrogatory and volatile. Yes, he was a shepherd from the Pyrenees, had been in the Foreign Legion, had been a criminal (I could see scars and tattoos even in the moonlight), was on pilgrimage through France. So who was I, and what was I about?

What indeed! I had about three seconds in which to flee or make friends. I decided to make friends. Within a few days we could be seen walking among the vineyards together, smoking terrible cheap cigars, in deep discussion. How was it possible with so little common ground? I was taking my first steps in engaging with otherness, taking on the different, and liking it.

So the word "shepherd" has particular associations for me of one who came my way at a particular moment of truth and confronted my fear of difference. It suggests someone utterly different from me, alarmingly foreign, challenging me to meet and enter into a relationship with him. I remember the shepherd knocking the packet of cigars out of my hand into the ditch to emphasize his point that I wasn't being honest in what I said. I think of the pleasure at discovering that my arms were meant for waving around too, not just for gripping umbrellas.

When it comes to thinking about Jesus as the Good Shepherd, these are very good associations to have. Jesus the stranger, the other, the one who comes not at our bidding as a genie from a lamp, not as one who suits us as we are, but as the different one who challenges us to engage with him and risk being changed. Until we have felt the force of Jesus' otherness and strangeness, real love cannot begin.

I think of that passage from Christopher Isherwood's novel, *The World in the Evening,* in which Stephen tells Elizabeth Rydal:

> Sometimes, though, you talked about love in a way that showed me you were remembering a personal experience. I can see you now, in the twilight of a winter afternoon, sitting with your fingertips stretched towards the fire, looking deeply into it, and saying, "No, Stephen; that's not how it begins—not by two people being drawn together. It's the moment when they suddenly know they're different from each other. Utterly, utterly different; so that it's horribly painful—unbearable almost. You're like the North and South Poles. You couldn't possibly be further apart. And yet, at the same time, you're more connected than any other two points on the surface of the earth. Because there's this axis between you. And everything else turns round it."[1]

This passage helps me understand what conversion is like. It is the moment of truth in which I discover that the Lord is holy, the Holy One—not at my disposal, not a projection of my wishes, not at all the God I had dreamed of having. We are utterly different, God and I. We couldn't possibly be further apart. But in conversion I find myself connected. There is an axis between us and everything else turns on it. And once I surrender the defensive theory that God is mere wish-fulfillment, then I make myself vulnerable to being met, touched, faced in precisely those ways I had dreaded, because they would begin a transformation I might not be able to limit.

Stories of conversion, simple or sophisticated, tell of this discovery of the axis between the self and the Holy One, and the fearful and wonderful recognition that the Other is free, active, and all initiative. The moment is celebrated in the moving poem that ends John Bowker's great book, *The Religious Imagination and the Sense of God:*

But what if the dream outlines the shape,
Creates what was there before the creation,
Imagines what was there to be imagined?
The earthquake in the soul
Splits the security of explanation.
My other self, my self, my other,
And love between, the correspondent fire;
The image made beyond, outside the self,
The print of otherness
With unexpected action of its own
And all initiative:
So rapt the feeling, some will feel it so,
I come like passionate lover to the soul
And rape the mystic on his bed of pain.[2]

The shocking, unacceptable image at the end jolts us into awareness that conversion is not the product of a negotiation, but encounter with the Other.

The same experience can come in all sorts of simple, earthy, and even humorous experiences. I asked a retreatant last week to imagine Christ in her prayer coming toward her along a beach. What would he say to her? What did he seem like? When she later gave an account of her meditation she spoke of her acute discomfort at finding Christ so unkempt, in dirty jeans and sneakers and with hair that was far from clean. The urge to tidy him up was almost irresistible until they both began to laugh. She found a most unusual sense of readiness to stay with him after that. Letting him be scruffy and casual was a symbol of letting Jesus be Jesus, letting go of the censorship imposed by her phony and defensive standards. You might smile a little at the apparent hokiness of this—but you wouldn't if you knew her and the sort of changes this symbolic encounter is heralding.

The prayer we do during Eastertide—encountering Christ in the stories of the resurrection appearances—has a particular quality I want to highlight. In Easter prayer our narcissism is placed under stress. Narcissism is one of the most prevalent forms of fallenness in our particular culture. One criterion becomes dominant: the criterion of what is "comfortable" for us. This plaintive word crops up everywhere: "I am not comfortable with this, I am not comfortable with that...." Once comfort becomes the test for reality, we risk imprisonment within the self. Encounter with otherness, engagement with what is strange and different, can seldom be comfortable. To love and let the other be other, to love the Holy One whose thoughts are not our thoughts and whose ways are not our ways, to learn from the Holy One the strange art of loving enemies—none of this can be comfortable. If you want comfort you had better seek it in the safely closed circle of your own self, contenting yourself with an existence that has all the appearance of life because of the intermittent ripples on the surface. But in reality you are merely blowing on the water for the satisfaction of seeing your own reflection again once the ripples subside.

In Easter prayer we are told that we can't control or predict or hold down or in any way dictate to the Lord who was not bound by death. He comes and he goes, as and when he chooses, in whatever guise and whatever place. Shutting the door won't keep him out. He appears for the most part as a stranger, someone who is other than the one we are used to and expect. By appearing as a stranger Christ tells us that love of him, love of the Father with whom he is one, is inseparable from the enterprise of engaging with the strange. Love of him is simply not compatible with the comfort we take in the familiar, the known, what we like and are like.

Often Eastertide is more profoundly about repentance and conversion than Lent is. We can all find sins and shortcomings to work on in Lent, but it is Easter that more starkly exposes the fear of loving and being loved that is at the root of our sin. Dare we engage with this free other, this Christ? What if this destroys our comfort, drawing us into action, relationship, community, hope, and the pain and glory of involvement in diversity, conflict, strangeness? We hesitate....

In Easter prayer we are placed in a fateful place of truth. Shall we shut the door out of fear? Or shall we feel around our shoulders the firm hold of the Shepherd's hands as we reply to the question, "Do you love me?" and hear the Shepherd's response, "Feed my sheep"?

Notes

1. Christopher Isherwood, *The World in the Evening* (New York: Avon Books, 1978), 83.

2. John Bowker, *The Religious Imagination and the Sense of God* (Oxford: Clarendon, 1978), 317.

The Converted Life

Lent, at the monastery

T he eighth chapter of John's gospel consists of a long discourse by Jesus that begins with the declaration, "I am
the light of the world." As invariably happens in this gospel,
Jesus' words provoke interrogation, controversy, and misunderstanding. But halfway through, when Jesus has proclaimed,
"When you have lifted up the Son of Man, then you will realize that I am he," the evangelist tells us that "as he was saying
these things, many believed in him."

The fourth gospel is an inexhaustible source of reflection on
the experience of conversion and in the eighth chapter we are
being asked to consider a particular kind of conversion: the experience of immediate conviction, the immediate onset of
faith. This experience is quite unlike what happens as a result
of deliberation and analysis. We are not told that some of Jesus' audience in the temple went home and had a discussion,
breaking up into small groups and then doing the first-century
equivalent of writing on newsprint the pros and cons of Jesus'
credibility. Nor did they go home to do some "journaling,"
personally investigating through meditation whether Jesus'
teaching seemed to fit where they were on their spiritual journey. No, these people were overtaken by an immediate sense
of Jesus' authenticity while he was still speaking, there and
then.

The words "as he saying these things, many believed in him" caught my attention in the reading of today's gospel because only a few days ago I had a very powerful religious experience in which I became conscious that a deep change had just occurred within me. My whole body, from the top of my head to the soles of my feet, registered an intense feeling of reordering and integration, of things slipping into place, the recognition of a new onset of truth and connection, the falling away of some barrier to inner communication, the untying of knots in the soul.

Just such an experience is suggested by the evangelist's comment. Right there in the temple the bodies of some of the listeners sense a flow of energy that expresses complete intuition of something that can be trusted through and through. "As he was saying these things, many believed in him." Before these listeners could analyze Jesus' words, they experienced wordlessly, through their bodies, "This is for real. Jesus is for real. What he is saying is for real. Where he is coming from is for real. What he says he is aiming for is for real. And I, as I take all this in, I am for real, more real than I have ever been before."

The other gospels tell us specifically that Jesus possessed an extraordinary authority quite unlike that of the legal experts. This question of authority is a key one for us in distinguishing true conversion from false. In some so-called conversions the flow of energy takes the form of abdicating one's authority and submitting to a hero-leader. Oh, what a thrill and a relief it is no longer to have to bear the burden of responsibility! The sheer exhilaration of no longer having to live creatively oneself and wrest meaning from the confusion of life! What a joy to let another decide, to have mastery! What a charge you get from belonging to a group that conspires to hand over all authority to a guru and leader! How good it feels simply to obey, parrot, submit, and proselytize! The shining eyes of cult members, the rapt smiles of converts, the calm certitude of disciples, all this tells us of the joys of abdication. But appearances are deceptive and the joys are as false as wax fruit.

If the authority Jesus possessed were simply yet another version of the magic by which one human being seduces others to abdicate their authority, what then? Authority is not necessarily a sign that one comes from God, not at all. But Jesus does not steal people's authority, forcing them to confer it upon him; instead, the people around Jesus find authority flowing into themselves. They participate in his authority, which is completely different from the seduction and abdication of false conversion.

Right at the beginning of his gospel John strikes this chord:

> He came to what was his own, and his own people did not accept him. But to all who received him, who believed in his name, he gave power to become children of God, who were born, not of blood or of the will of the flesh or of the will of man, but of God. (John 1:11-13)

He gave power to become children of God. This translation can be questioned because the Greek word, *exousia*, rendered here as "power," is translated everywhere else as "authority": "He gave them authority to become children of God." He gave them authority like his own to be in this world as he is. And those of course are no mere exaggerated words of my own, for the writer of the first letter of John was to say, "As he is, so are we in this world" (4:17).

Now I think it is obvious to most of us that the icon of Jesus painted by John in his gospel is not a naturalistic rendering. The other gospel writers also created distinctive impressions of Jesus with an artistry wholly unlike modern biography or journalism. But John has taken the boldest steps away from reportage into the creative realm, using distortion and selectivity and elaboration with shocking freedom. What we recognize as some of the most emphatic features of John's portrait of Jesus are, I believe, the very features that we ourselves will acquire through conversion. John has Jesus continually return to certain themes so that we can see as in a mirror the new features of our own converted lives.

Three very prominent characteristics of John's portrait of Jesus are as instantly recognizable as the elongations and storminess of an El Greco painting. The first is an intense awareness of being sent by God. The theme of phrases such as "this is the will of the One who sent me" resound again and again. Jesus is fulfilling his mission as sent from God and then he will return to the One who sent him. But the intensity and saturation of this coloring of all Jesus' words and actions with the sense of "sentness" is not meant to separate us from him, and thus degrade our discipleship by comparison. The opposite is true. The believer in Jesus gains in conversion exactly the same conviction of having been given life and of being brought into the world to fulfill a mission from God. When Jesus anoints the sightless eyes of the blind man with mud he commands him to wash his eyes clear in the pool of Siloam, which the evangelist points out means "sent."

The new vision that comes with conversion brings with it the gift of a sense that one's life is purposeful, that one has been given a mission, a life-task for God. Perhaps we who have been Christians from childhood tend to take all this for granted, but we must realize how many people flounder in the world with the feeling that their lives are purely accidental, that any sense of purpose is merely a fiction to give some kind of consistency to a life that is nothing more than the accidental product of biological and social forces. But new converts can tell us of the radical change that comes when they undergo the experience that John represents in the scene of the Risen Christ in the upper room: "As the Father has sent me, so I send you."

The second and intimately related feature of John's icon of Jesus is agency. Jesus knows what he is doing and when it is time to do it, and he knows that he is doing it. We can be pretty sure that this is based on actual memories of Jesus, and

Mark's austere image of him steadily walking to Jerusalem ahead of his baffled disciples shows that an indelible impression was made on those who saw him. But the icon of Jesus in John radiates this sense of agency, timing, and ownership of his actions. He is very wary of his mother's interference at Cana in case she throws off his own sense of the right time for his action. All the way through, Jesus' words emphasize his own authority and responsibility for his actions, culminating in his emphatic repudiation of the role of impotent victim:

> For this reason the Father loves me, because I lay down my life in order to take it up again. No one takes it from me, but I lay it down of my own accord. I have power to lay it down, and I have power to take it up again. (John 10:17-18)

Now it is just this sense of agency and responsibility that comes as a gift from God in the converted life. In profane life, human beings suffer from a sense that not only are their lives accidental, but the fate to which they must resign themselves is that of being forever pushed around, manipulated, and dictated to. In the converted life, we are endowed with responsibility and with power.

In John's gospel there is a terrific emphasis on believing, knowing, and abiding, but there is an equal emphasis on doing:

> Very truly, I tell you, the one who believes in me will also do the works that I do and, in fact, will do greater works than these, because I am going to the Father. (John 14:12)

The life of the convert feels neither reactive nor impotent, but purposeful and fruitful: "I appointed you to go and bear fruit" (15:16). Of course discipleship means passion too—suffering, being acted upon. Christ says to Peter that he will be taken where he does not want to go. But this will be an expression of the voluntary dying of the seed, which must fall into the ground before bearing fruit.

The third feature of John's gospel, which blends into the other two, is that of centeredness. Andras Angyal, in his great book, *Neurosis and Treatment,* declares:

> To be is to mean something to someone else. This existence is something we cannot create for ourselves: it can only be given us by another. All we have is a profound urge to exist and the dreadful sense of non-existence. A poem written in a language that no one can read does not exist as a poem. Neither do we exist in a human way unless someone decodes us.

The Jesus of John's gospel can say "I am" so powerfully because he is totally understood and known by God. He is so known by God that he is in the Father and the Father is in him. And this is the authority that comes to us as converted believers. If I know myself to be utterly known, utterly known and completely loved, then I *am.* I really am. I really exist. I mean everything to God and therefore my life has meaning.

What Shall We
Do For Lent?

S hrove Tuesday calls us to think about sin in preparation
for the season of repentance, yet the tradition of revelry
associated with Mardi Gras militates against deadly seriousness. Can we let ourselves into the subject of sin a little lightly?

Ogden Nash has a delightful poem called "Portrait of the
Artist as a Prematurely Old Man" that explores comically the
classic distinction between sins of commission and sins of
omission. He warns us not to bother our heads about the first
kind, "because however sinful, they must at least be fun or
else you wouldn't be committing them." It is through the sins
of omission that we get bitten. These are the things that "lay
eggs under our skin." Their "painful lack of beauty" consists in
that fact that we

> ...didn't get a wicked forbidden thrill
> Every time you let a policy lapse or forgot to pay a bill;
> You didn't slap the lads in the tavern on the back
>   and loudly cry Whee
> Let's all fail to write just one more letter before
>   we go home, and this round of unwritten letters is on me.
> No, you never get any fun

Out of the things you haven't done,
But they are the things I do not like to be amid,
Because the suitable things you didn't do
   give you a lot more trouble
   than the unsuitable things you did.
The moral is that it is probably better not to sin at all,
   but if some kind of sin you must be pursuing,
Well, remember to do it by doing rather than by not doing.[1]

You know, there is more insight beneath the surface of Nash's jocularity than in the earnest sermons of many a Christian moralist.

What we do wrong is often less harmful than our failure to do good. Our wrongdoing is so often powered by an energy that can be converted to good. Our aggression is misdirected when we use it to put others down, but aggression can be transfigured when we use it to track down and cut out from our lives what is false and inimical to love. The secret of sin does not lie in our energetic but misdirected action; it lies in our inertia and forgetfulness, in our inner deadness, denial, and boredom. The secret of hell lies in our not loving, in our not risking, in our withholding. Evil is our paralysis in the face of love's invitation, our great refusal.

W. H. Auden put his finger on it in his poem, "In Memory of Sigmund Freud." Freud, he wrote, went his way

Down among the Lost People like Dante, down
   To the stinking fosse where the injured
   Lead the ugly life of the rejected
And showed us what evil is: not as we thought
Deed that must be punished, but our lack of faith,
   Our dishonest mood of denial,
   The concupiscence of the oppressor.[2]

In Lent we will all do well to look at what we do and see what needs changing and converting in our behavior. We will do well to focus on some of our typical acts that it is high time we curbed or dropped, so that the energy behind them can fuel good actions and more life-enhancing behavior. But if this is what we think repentance is, we shall be heading for disillusionment. No repentance goes deep enough that fails to penetrate the core of our inertia, our faithless numbness.

One of the earliest snatches of Christian hymnody in the letter to the Ephesians tells us what the essence of repentance is: "Sleeper, awake! Rise from the dead, and Christ will shine on you" (5:14). Through the resurrection of Christ we can awake from paralysis and inertia. Easter embraced can waken our desire for life and for God the giver of life, and our capacity for the kind of giving that does not deplete but enlivens. In Lent the church says to us, "Before hearing the good news of the resurrection again, taste the reality of your need again, experience your deadness. Then hear the voice of Christ arousing you from sleep."

Lent is not a temporary affectation of gloom or a brisk interlude for self-improvement. It is for being in the wilderness, which means stopping long enough to recognize the truth of our inertia and faithlessness. This deadness inside is a fact. On Ash Wednesday we are called first to face this fact—but then what? What shall we do?

This may seem strange, but this year every time I have asked myself the question "What shall I do for Lent?" I have immediately thought of a brief exchange that occurs in a droll Russian novel by Goncharov. The hero, Oblomov, is asked what he does. The question astonishes and offends him. "What? What do I do? Why, I am in love with Olga!" To him, the question about what he does is a question about his identity. He is a man in love, and that is who he understands himself to be. It would be a betrayal to answer the question as it was posed. He answers instead the question he should have been asked.

The question that should be put to us all at the beginning of Lent is not "What shall we do?" The right question is the one to which the answer is, "Why, I am in love with God!" What begins to enliven our inertia is remembering and realizing that we are in love with God. I wonder how you feel about saying "I am in love with God"? I suspect if you were to utter these words quietly it would not be long before you became aware of voices from within contradicting and ridiculing you. "The hell you are! You're not in love with God. How dare you be so pretentious?...Fine lover you are!...Fancy yourself a mystic, do you?"

These voices have a certain ring of truth. Even the greatest saints are overwhelmed from time to time with the sense that they haven't even begun to love. The trouble is these voices insist on being the only ones to have a say. They drown out the other voice from a deep place within us that, in spite of everything, is ready to return the love of God.

These voices become our enemies when they bully and oppress us into believing that we are hopeless non-starters. They can stultify us, pressing us back down into our mediocrity and telling us we belong there. These are not the voices of penitence, these voices that tell us that we are inadequate and hypocritical. They are the voices that kill repentance.

True repentance, true change of heart, consists in grasping the fact that we are called to be in love with God, and that the love with which we love God is something already given to us. Repentance is believing that "the love of God has been poured into our hearts through the Holy Spirit that has been given to us" and that this love flows back to God. Repentance is trusting that we are entitled to be in love with God, because this is a state that is given us, something we have received by grace through faith. Repentance is coming alive to our given identity as lovers of God.

So, what shall we do for Lent? We shall act on our identity as women and men who are in love with God. We shall do whatever helps us remember and realize that identity and do what arises from it. We shall pray more regularly, at greater leisure, because in prayer we identify ourselves to God as lovers and dare to feel our way into this role.

In the wonderful Wesley hymn "O thou who camest from above" there is a reference to prayer in very traditional language, "my acts of faith and love repeat." Acts of prayer are those utterances of trust and love, of which the simplest example is, "God, I love you."

Modern people are usually suspicious of this word "act." To encourage us to make *acts* of faith and love seems to suggest that we make insincere declarations, saying things that are not really true. This accursed demand for sincerity is ready to strangle any new-born love in its cradle because it is not yet fully grown and mature. Our acts of faith and love are new-born beginnings, not words of hypocrisy. In prayer we cherish them in their weakness and smallness, believing that they will grow in time, if nourished and given freedom.

Lent is for spiritual combat. Whenever you hear the voices that say, "You can't tell God about your love because you don't mean it, you are just pretending," tell them to go to hell where they came from. Here is what to do for Lent. Find time tomorrow to tell God of your love and faith. If you have to, tell the voices of inertia and self-doubt to go to hell. Then the day after, tell God again—and the day after that. When Easter comes and we cry our Alleluias together, we shall know a little better than we did that it is true. God has won our love, and by grace through faith we can know ourselves to be in love.

Notes
1. Ogden Nash, *Verses from 1929 On* (New York: The Modern Library, 1956), 16.
2. W. H. Auden, *Collected Works* (New York: Random House, 1945), 163.

A Strange and Foolish Story

The Conversion of Paul, at the monastery

W hen I was a novice in our community, the Society of St. John the Evangelist, in England, I remember reading an article by an expert on resources for evangelism. The author was able to commend certain sources for written materials but he also had some scathing remarks about certain organizations whose contributions were pitiful. Since I like sarcasm, I was enjoying these withering criticisms until I came to the following sentence:

> Then there was that Society, from whose title one might have assumed a certain interest in evangelism, which, when asked to send samples of literature that it published, sent me a thin pile of pamphlets, with yellow pages and rusted staples. The first one was a booklet teaching soldiers in the First World War how to pray the Rosary.

I blushed with instant recognition. The object of ridicule was none other than my own community! I could see it now: our Superior had received this inquiry and passed it on to old Father Wilks, who had obediently collected samples of all the tracts that had been quietly moldering in the cabinet for decades.

We are a Society whose name gives people every right to assume that we are interested in evangelism. How do we contribute to evangelism? How do we, and how do you? And what goes on in evangelism?

Let's explore some basics. First, the word itself is indispensable. True, it is encrusted with terrible associations drawn both from fundamentalism and triumphalism, in which the proud possessors of absolute truth hand it on to the benighted. We would like to start again with an unsoiled word. But like that other battered and defiled word, *God*, we can't do without it. Christianity communicates through narrative and grows by storytelling. In all its rites, sacraments, preaching, and teaching it continually tells a story—about the preparation for and the coming of Jesus, and about Jesus' death and resurrection. No religions are without stories, but Christianity is uniquely bound up with a story it announces as *news*. Buddhists do not evangelize; instead, they induct seekers into a spiritual path. Islam propagates itself not through evangelism, but by assimilating people into a total practice of devotion and obedience embodied in the Koran.

We are more aware than ever that the story Christians tell is one story among others. Down through the ages similar stories have been told of dying and rising gods, and the story of Jesus seems like another version, if a peculiar one. There are many hero stories and salvation myths around which communities have held themselves together, not unlike the way the Christian churches make their identity from the gospel story. However, Christians can never tell the story of Jesus as just one story among others without falling into self-contradiction, because for them it is not an interesting alternative to other stories, but *the* story.

Nowadays the instant you say that, hackles rise. Christians are nervous about repeating their bad history of cultural and religious imperialism and want to do justice to the saving grace inherent in other religions practiced by God's beloved children. One Episcopal diocesan convention recently refused to pass a motion saying that Christ was the way, the truth, and the life; it was amended to Christ is *a* way, *a* truth, and *a* life. That kind of modern political correctness almost tempts one to laugh, but we need to recognize that people are trying to compensate for a sinful past of triumphalism. The effort has the effect of pushing Christians over into contradiction. Something as essential as the spine itself is being removed in this surgical operation upon the Christian story.

The Christian story contains a simple and intrinsic claim. It claims to be potentially the story of everyone. Christians are prevented by the inner logic of the story from ever saying to anyone, "Because you are already committed to this religion or that, this story is not intended for you. Because your culture or spirituality is so worthy of preservation, or your philosophy so honorable, this story is not meant for you. It is only for us." Instead it has to say, "This is a story that all human beings are entitled to hear and make their own." Christians must not say, "You have to accept this story because every other source of spiritual meaning is garbage." What we must say is that this is a story to which every human being has the right of access.

Evangelism does not mean Christians telling one another the story in re-confirmation and celebration of the meaning it already has for us. Evangelism happens when Christians tell the story in the presence of others who have not yet found it to be their story. There are those for whom the Christian story is one story among others, in some aspects a good story, but still only one of many windows into reality. Then there are those who appreciate the Christian story precisely as the story belonging to Christians. That is, the story appears meaningful and attractive and they can see that it works in the lives of Christians in community, but they themselves remain outside the story. It has not become their own story or unlocked the meaning of their own history. We engage in evangelism when we tell the story in such a way that it gives the listener the chance to hear it as her own story, his own story.

What is necessary in the evangelist for this chance, this opportunity, to be created? Certainly not sophistication or eloquence. Paul helps us be clear on that. The gospel is a strange and foolish story, and eloquence and elaborate arguments to press its cogency actually go against the grain of the story itself. The story is about a vulnerable God who is more on the side of erring human beings than they are themselves, and who gives himself up to be one of them and die as one of them, for all of them. This story of the weakness and foolishness of God is a story that can be told by weak and foolish people in their own particular way because its force does not depend on human powers of rhetoric and wisdom. But there is one qualification. If we engage in evangelism we intend to give the hearers the chance to make their story their own, and we can't do that unless we show in the telling that we have made the story our own as well.

Telling someone the story—the story cherished by the church—is never quite enough to be the catalyst for conversion. In the chemistry there has to be personal witness, the capacity to show that the story you are telling is *your* story. You are able to tell the story of your own life in terms of the gospel, as an illustration and example of it. In the seaside resorts of England a traditional candy is sold, long cylinders of bright pink rock-hard candy, with the name of the resort embedded throughout the whole length so in every piece the name can be read. The labels always say, "Lettered all through." In Christians who evangelize there is an awareness that no matter which way you slice your life into stories, the pattern of God's grace can be read from it.

Maybe this then is the answer to the question of how the Society is involved with the work of evangelism. We do have personal contact with those to whom the story of Jesus means nothing, but they are few. Much more we are in a position to help hundreds and hundreds of believers appropriate the story, make it their own, and read their own lives as stories of grace, "lettered all through" with the gospel. And thus we help to empower them to be evangelists, able to give others a chance to hear the story and make it their own, as they hear it from the lips of those who are not mere narrators, but witnesses.

Maybe you don't think of yourself as an evangelist, but you can prepare for that opportunity by learning to be bolder in telling the stories of God that embody your own. Are you prepared to tell stories from your own life that speak of the gospel of a suffering and gracious God who is more on your side than you are? Stories of appropriation, those moments when the reality of grace came home to you? Stories of intensification, those times that deepened the impression of the gospel on your life? And stories of conversion, those turning points when things changed forever?

Today we celebrate the Conversion of Paul, a feast day for celebrating the power of personal stories to bear witness to the gospel. The book of Acts has Paul tell the story in full three times. He probably told it a thousand times. Think of all that comes home to us in Paul's story. The way in which God comes into our lives by calling us by name: "I am called, therefore I am." The grief and frustration, the patience and the perseverance of Christ in the face of our resistance to the good news of the foolishness and weakness of God in the cross. The change that comes over us when we suddenly grasp that Christ is not a distant divine figure but a living presence keeping intimate company with the ordinary, simple, suffering people who let him into their lives.

"Why are you persecuting me?" In this one question the whole gospel is present. It is the appeal of a loving Savior who is completely identified with those he calls his own and who is with them in everything, everywhere, and forever so that he can bring them to where he is, alive on the other side of death. Your stories have the same signs embedded in them if only you would realize it and practice telling them.

Passing Over

Threshold

The profession of life vows by Curtis Almquist, SSJE,
and Carl Winter, SSJE, at the monastery

E ver since our prehistoric ancestors made magic signs at
the threshold of a newly found cave to gain courage to
enter in, human beings have appreciated the need for rituals
to help us move on and move in. Times come in life when
preparation and initiation are over. We are at a threshold; our
community asks us, "Will you step through?" It offers us a ritual that will help us cross over.

Since the beginning of the summer I have been meditating
on a particular monastic building that tells us what it means to
cross the kind of threshold that Carl and Curtis are now standing at. It is an ancient Buddhist shrine at Braga in the Himala-
yas, beneath the great mountain Annapurna. In the inner
chamber are hundreds of wooden statues of *boddhisatvas,*
those compassionate human beings of Buddhist mythology
who consent to thousands of reincarnations in order to assist
others toward enlightenment. Those who have entered this inner chamber say that the faces of the images radiate compassion. But before pilgrims enter the inner room they have to
pass right under a terrifying image, repulsive beyond words:
the *vajrapani,* a loathsome figure dripping with blood and fes-
tooned with skulls.

The poet David Whyte can take us all there in his beautiful
poem, "The Faces at Braga":

In monastery darkness
by the light of one flashlight
the old shrine room waits in silence.

While above the door
we see the terrible figure,
fierce eyes demanding. "Will you step through?"

And the old monk leads us,
bent back nudging blackness
prayer beads in the hand that beckons.[1]

Why the terrible figure in the holy place? It is there to make sure we face our fear, to make us take our fear with us into the holy place. To shock us out of our tendency to keep our fear down, unfelt and hidden. In the darkness the light suddenly flashes on the hideous image and our fear leaps up into our throats from its hiding place. At this point the old monk beckons us; we are now ready to pass inside.

In Christian churches the threshold at the west end was often under a vast tableau of the Last Judgment. The purpose was the same, to shock us out of amnesia, to remind us of the risk of ruin, to make us remember what we dread. And what is the first thing visitors see in this monastery church of ours? The crucifix, the figure of the crucified, a terrible sight, this reminder of pain and savagery, a tortured man bleeding and suffering to death.

These ritual spaces are telling us that we cannot enter into the holy place without encountering our fear and bringing it with us. This is what lies at the heart of initiation into the religious life. We have tried to make sure that Curtis and Carl have met what is fearful and that they bring it with them. Curtis tells me that he has been using sleeping pills for the first time ever this week, and Carl has been looking a bit haggard, so all is going according to plan. They are afraid.

The vows hold us in the places where we need to meet our deepest fears. There is the vow of poverty. Who among us does not dread nothingness, emptiness, futility? In the middle ages one of the first books a novice had to read was the book of Ecclesiastes, with its implacable voicing of our worst suspicions—that "vanity of vanity, all is vanity." We are afraid that we are empty inside and that at the end of our lives there will be nothing to show for our striving.

Monasticism seeks to heighten this anxiety by getting us to relinquish ownership of many of the things that assuage it: prospects of career success, a solid home, consoling possessions. It pushes us nearer the edge where we are forced to look over and ask, "Where is my true center, my real substance and wealth?" Our founder, Father Benson, used to say, "Think of the religious life not as a mode of living for God, but a mode in which God would live in you."

When we are at this critical edge we make a discovery that is simple but crucial: God dwells in us. We are filled with the fullness of God. Then the paradox of St. Paul, "as having nothing, and yet possessing everything," seems just the simple truth. "All belong to you, and you belong to Christ, and Christ belongs to God." We make a vow of poverty because we have found that Life itself, the author of life, lives in us. And yet this discovery is not secure; it is not another possession. Our fear of nothingness crouches at the door and it is only by a repeated exploration in faith that we find that the pearl of great price is still there in our hearts.

There is the vow of celibacy. Who among us has not felt the fear of sterility and impotence? The fear that the passion within us will never be fully aroused or it will go to seed? The dread that we won't find a great love in our life but simply join the masses that trudge the way, if not of quiet desperation, of resignation? The fear that we will not create new life and pass it on? Monasticism intensifies the fear by taking us away from the path which most human beings follow, the finding of a spouse or lover, the creation of a family or partnership. It disconnects us from these opportunities of fulfillment and then says, "Now find the great love of your life!" And some of us do. "Think of the religious life not as a mode of living for God, but as a mode in which God would live in you." God lives in us and we find that we are among the number of those whose lives find meaning and fruitfulness from a great love. We find the Spirit welling up as love in us. We find Christ in us choosing us and inviting our free choice. The Father lives in us, evoking a love with no restraints.

There is the vow of obedience. Who has not felt the fear of not being heard, of not counting or mattering? The dread of that isolation in which one's actions are inconsequential? The religious life intensifies the dread by bringing you into community, where it seems that others will have power over you and rob you of initiative and responsibility. But "think of the religious life not as a mode for living for God, but as a mode in which God would live in you."

The new religious realizes that the Spirit lives in him as Creator Spirit, fostering his own creativity and giving him a full voice. The community, in all its fragility and humanness, is experienced as the dwelling of the Spirit and we realize that the common life of mutual accountability and reciprocal regard is what we really long for. It is a great joy to hear and be heard, to take seriously and be taken seriously, to affirm and be affirmed, to challenge and be challenged in the power of the same Spirit who dwells in each and in all.

So we pause at the threshold, making sure that Carl and Curtis feel the futility, barrenness, and isolation we all dread. And then we cross over and pass within. Let us again follow the poet as he leads us into the shrine room at Braga to see the images within.

> Such love in solid wood!
> Taken from the hillsides and carved in silence
> they have the vibrant stillness of those who made them.

...Carved in devotion
their eyes have softened through age
and their mouths curve through delight of the carver's hand.

If only our own faces
would allow the invisible carver's hand
to bring the deep grain of love to the surface.

If only we knew,
as the carver knew, how the flaws
in the wood led his searching chisel to the very core,

we would smile too
and not need faces immobilized
by fear and the weight of things undone.

When we fight with our failing
We ignore the entrance to the shrine itself
and wrestle with the guardian,
fierce figure on the side of good.[2]

From the statues the pilgrims learn the meaning of transformation, the goal of all our pilgrimages and the fundamental purpose of monastic life. "Such love in solid wood!" The statues smile through delight of the carver's hand. This smile tells us what it means to accept that we are not our own makers: we are being made, being formed and transformed. The secret is a surrender; only God, not we ourselves, can bring the deep grain of love to the surface.

"Think of the religious life as the mode in which God would live in you." Live in you so as to transform and shape you from one degree of glory to another. If only our own faces would allow the carving hand of God "to bring the deep grain of love to the surface." If only we could give ourselves to the blows of the carver's hand. To give ourselves up to transformation we need to know something. "If only we knew, as the carver knew, how the flaws in the wood led his searching chisel to the very core." The statues are cracked, flawed, knotted, bent. Yet through these very faults and flaws the carver has penetrated to the inmost grain. The statues smile because their flaws have been used and transfigured by the carver, Love and Compassion itself.

When we don't know this, or we forget it, monastic life can become as grim as any other way of life in which we make ourselves our own maker, when we "fight with our failing" instead of giving ourselves up to the carver's hands.

Curtis and Carl, we don't let the starry-eyed take vows for life. We invite you to step over this threshold because you know that this community is not an elite corps. You know how cracked and flawed we are, and how doomed to fail, how tense is the effort to fight our failing. Cross the threshold and join us as ones who think of the religious life not as a way of living for God, but as a way God lives in us. Join us as those who have surrendered the attempt to make yourselves right, make yourselves perfect. Step inside as those who know that our wounds, our absurdities, our cracks and blemishes and rotten parts are flaws that lead the searching chisel of the carver of Nazareth to the core of our being. Enter in as those who yield the initiative for transformation to the Risen One who lives in you. Step through, aware of what you dread, so he may be your hope. Come in as flawed men whose only desire is for the invisible carver's hand to bring the deep grain of love to the surface. Come in and grow younger with us toward death.

Notes

1. David Whyte, "The Faces at Braga," from *Where Many Rivers Meet* (Langley, Wash.: Many Rivers Press), 1990.
2. Ibid.

Lover of Souls

The ordination to the priesthood of Eldridge Pendleton, SSJE,
on St. Andrew's Day, at the monastery

One of the reasons I miss my journeys to the community's house in North Carolina is that I was always eager to see what Eldridge, the incorrigible curator and collector, had rescued from some obscure junk shop or yard sale and installed in the house after careful restoration. One month a carved chair, another a pair of matching cruets. We will never get the antiquarian out of Eldridge so we might as well sit back and enjoy it as part of his wonderful character and humanity that God is pleased to consecrate and bless in making him a priest.

Jesus showed his sympathy to collectors by making them an image of the scribe in the kingdom of heaven, who brings forth from his treasure things old and things new. And I think on this occasion we could pay tribute to this feature of Eldridge's character by visiting the church's attic and retrieving from its dusty recesses something neglected and unfashionable about the office of priesthood. Oh yes, the church has an attic to which worn-out and outmoded theologies, symbols, and rites are relegated. Some of them are eventually fetched back out into the light of day, repaired, refinished, and burnished for the appreciation of a new generation.

Here is a very dented and tarnished phrase which once upon a time was used to pay tribute to good priests, especially in obituaries. Of a good priest it used to be said that he was a "lover of souls." Merely to pronounce the words these days invites snorts of derision; to our modern ears it sounds absurdly disembodied, as if priests attended to wraiths and abstractions rather than flesh-and-blood human beings. If we were to rescue this expression it would need a lot of restoration, a lot of polishing. Shall we give it a try?

The first thing to ask is whether we have found an ideal replacement for "lover of souls." Can we do without it? Let's try some alternatives. We can skip over "lover of bodies" right away as a lurid irony, reminding us precisely of the prevalent sexual abuse by ministers that has resulted from forgetfulness of soul. So let us try "lover of persons, lover of people." This will do perfectly, won't it? The priest is called to love people *as* people, to love their persons, their embodied selves, their selves in relation. We could have a ball expounding this expression, for who among us does not believe that concern with persons is at the heart of the gospel? But the more you repeat the phrase, the more you realize that it is a phrase of our liberal, late twentieth-century culture, a phrase especially of our therapeutic culture. Soon we realize that there is nothing distinctive enough about this phrase for it to be applied to Christian priests. There are countless therapists, activists, movers and shakers, artists and social workers who are equally moved by a profound love of persons. Innumerable humanists and virtuous unbelievers and atheists love people and care for persons while not caring at all for the metaphysical fictions and illusions they believe religion to consist of.

Perhaps then we are driven back to our phrase "lover of souls" if only for the reason that it is not a stock phrase equally applicable in the many healing professions. A priest loves souls, and this cannot be said in the same way of the community activist and the therapist. We had better ask, then, what "soul" means, and what makes "soul" the object of the priest's love. Put very simply, "soul" is the sound we make when we want to point in faith to a human being's capacity for intimacy and union with God. Soul is our intrinsic human capacity to be indwelt by the divine presence. To say "soul" is to say that you believe that this capacity for God is not a mysterious privilege attained by mystics or saints, but something that belongs to created human nature, something every human being has and is as it comes forth from the womb.

Now soul is known only to faith; persons and characters and relationships are right there before our eyes. There is an endless stream of evidence for the psyche, for the natural inner human life. We know about psyche—we don't have to believe in it. But soul is accessible only to faith, and the spirituality of priesthood is a sustained act of faith in soul, in the intrinsic capacity of each human being to be filled with all the fullness of God. The priest loves that in us even when we don't know we have that capacity, even when we deny it or forget it.

The priest as lover of souls takes a baby into her arms and loves that little creature, not merely as a cute little thing, but as a mystery greater than any angel, as one who is capable even now, as the water is poured into the font, of being indwelt by God the Holy Spirit. The priest stands with the body and blood of Christ in his hands and loves our souls, that emptiness, that space, that need, that openness in each man, woman, and child who stretches out hands to receive those gifts. The priest loves that in us even when we who are lining up are aware only of fretfulness, doubt, and distraction. The priest loves us in our souls, our capacity for sacramental union with Christ. The priest bends over the bed of the confused old lady near death who is aware of faith only as a memory of what she once had and is overwhelmed by fear. The priest loves her soul when the body is almost destroyed by disease, loves the soul she is not aware of but which is growing greater in the ordeal of the dark night by the grace of God, the soul which is made perfect in weakness.

The priest knows that preaching has a hundred ways of doing good by teaching and inspiring, cheering and uplifting and judging, but as a lover of souls the priest can never be content unless the word "pierces until it divides soul from spirit, joints from marrow," as the writer to the Hebrews put it. As a lover of souls he needs to find a word that penetrates to the point in which we distinguish our regular needs for consolation from the great need, the primal need, for reconciliation with God and union with God in love. We human beings tend to agree on what we need in order to cope—but the world around us, our families and friends, and even we ourselves, lend little support to that obscure and vulnerable secret deep down in us, that nothing less than oneness with God will fulfill our desire.

To the priest who is a lover of souls, this secret is no secret. The priest knows our desire, though we dread accepting it. So the priest goes up to the pulpit as a lover of souls, loving that obscure desire for God in us, though we often do not love it ourselves, and, whether we can bear it or not, tries to find a word of hope, of promise, that has good news for that desire.

The priest is a lover of what is real but unseen, unclear. To the priest who is a true lover of souls will come hundreds of people to make confession of sin and receive absolution. For we all have largely unseen lives of folly and betrayal, of apathy and faithlessness, and we will not lay them bare for the healing sacramental work of Christ except in the company of one who loves soul, loves the unseen we can hardly bear to have exposed to the light. The priest as a lover of souls is ready to love the raggedness and stink of our secret lives, knowing that they at first conceal, and then reveal, the presence of the crucified and risen Christ within us, who justifies us through faith in his blood.

Eldridge, God has been working all your life to prepare you for this moment and I know you are overwhelmed when you think about all the influences of people, places, and events that have converged to make you ready for this. Sometimes God pushes the young into priesthood; I am one of those. Others God leads through cumulative experiences of life so that they can take into their priesthood all that has gone before. Priesthood comes to you—how shall I put it delicately?—in life's afternoon. In some ways you will find, like the wedding guests at Cana, that the best wine has been served last in your life. In others ways you will wonder just how you got stuck with it. For from this day forward your life is ordained as a sign of the priestly character of the people of God. In your short time as a deacon you have experienced a little of what it means to be a sacramental sign of the servanthood of the Christian people. And now you are ordained a sign of the priesthood of the whole body. It is not something you can toy with and then put down. This is who you are until you die.

Years will go by and you will often be baffled by what priesthood is. What is unique to it? What are its special responsibilities? At a time when ministry is seen as the vocation of all the baptized, there will be many voices that will try to minimize or professionalize priesthood. But I think you will resist them, and your sense of what priesthood is will expand over the years, not contract, as you sense what it means to be a sign and embodiment for all of the priesthood that belongs to all.

Today, we have struck just one note by thinking of the old-fashioned expression "lover of souls." When you die, I hope people will say that this is what you have been as a priest, a man who lived with his eye on the unseen depth that lies beneath the surface of every person, of every moment. A priest who loved the invisible heart and soul, and was ready to touch it at any opportunity with the good news of Christ's universal presence and inexhaustible love.

Like a Peg in a Secure Place

The profession of initial vows by Brian Willmer, SSJE,
at the monastery

T his event has been in the forefront of my mind and heart for a long time. A few weeks ago I walked up the River Ribble from my parent's house to the ruins of Sawley Abbey to pray for Brian in a place where, as boys, both I, and later he, had often sat and felt the pull of monastic life. Later, in Spain, while staying at the ancient abbey of Lleyre, I had a day of retreat that I decided to devote to finding the words to say today as Brian enters into his initial vows. Mists were rolling down the limestone crags as they do in Chinese scroll paintings, but I saw a sign pointing up the hillside that read *Fuente San Virilar,* St. Virilar's Spring. Now I like to explore holy wells and springs, so I set off along the path leading into a maze of boxwood groves clinging to the hillside. I would seek a word at the spring of St. Virilar, whoever he was.

It was not long before I was saying to myself, "This is how people get lost!" Indeed, my companion who tried the path several days later in bright sunlight lost his way completely and had to come back down. I learned that St. Virilar was a ninth-century abbot who was remembered precisely because one day he got lost in the very maze of boulders and bushes through which I was threading an uncertain way. He was a man with one great question and many doubts surrounding it. He struggled to make sense of eternity, of how we could share in eternal life, of how one day in God's sight is as a thousand years, and a thousand years as one day. Here in these woods he heard a nightingale and followed it up the hillside. He knew he was hopelessly lost but he had to stay there by the spring, spellbound by the beauty of the bird's music.

When the nightingale stopped singing he somehow found a way back down to the monastery. But as he approached it, something was not right. The buildings were vastly changed and expanded, and the monks' habits were white, not black. The porter was a stranger. When he told them who he was, the monastery archivist was sent to look up the ancient records. There it was: three hundred years previously, one abbot Virilar was recorded missing and presumed dead. The story ends by his being welcomed into the monastery, now Cistercian.

This wonderful legend tells us that God answers our questions, answers the question that is each person's life, by leading us astray. It is very important, it is *essential*, that we get lost. It is our only hope. And when God answers that question through the monastic life, it is the outcome of getting thoroughly lost.

There are three losses. The first loss, common to all converts to Christ, is to wander off "the broad path" that Christ spoke of, that great highway thronged with people that leads to nowhere. We find ourselves on narrower paths without the security of belonging to a comfortable majority.

The second loss is when we lose "their way." Our families, schools, parishes, country, and heritage constrain us. They seem to require that we follow a certain path, that we have this kind of career, this kind of family, these kinds of aims. And somehow all this is lost on us. It just doesn't do anything for us. We can't get going. It can be very lonely and very strange to feel unfit for all that, unready for it, not attracted by it.

Then there is a third loss. When we are really lost we say to ourselves, "I have lost my way." "My way" is the idea I fabricate for myself of the path. I tell my soul, "So the usual and general ways are not for me. Well then, I will follow my vocation in this way—first I will go here, then I will join this, and the way it will work out is...." I imagine monastic life, but I shape it on my terms. Then God makes all my plans go awry, become unworkable, and deprives me of "my way." He evicts us from the house of our own making. But if we consent to be completely lost, then God lets us find the way. Quite suddenly, we find our place.

The maze is an image our monastic ancestors built into many of their churches as a sign of the blessed hope of being lost, so that we can be found by God. At the abbey of Lleyre the maze is a hillside and it was not surprising that I should think of Brian there, who in a decade has gone round the monastic maze twice before. Upon my return from Spain I asked Brian what he had been praying about on his retreat and he replied, "About the maze I have been threading my way through in my life. I even retraced my footsteps in the sand as if following a maze." At a seeming dead-end in his life a little bird suggested a visit to our community in Cambridge, and although it was hardly as alluring a sound as the song of the nightingale, he was willing to follow it. As it turns out, his time with us was a reemergence from the maze that was a bit like St. Virilar's—into a community with a different habit, a community that loved him at once and is still a little in awe of the divine providence that has led him to us as a gift and a joy.

I finally arrived at the spring, a trickle from the rock in a deep bower, and sat there in the silence of the mist to listen for a word. All at once I recalled a saying of the prophet Isaiah that had struck me in the previous Sunday's readings: "I will fasten him like a peg in a secure place." This word expresses the other side of the mystery of the religious vocation. On the one hand, this vocation is a way, a movement, a pilgrimage, a straight course to God. On the other, it is a stability, an abiding, a staying, a taking root. There is a wonderful expression that comes to us from the monastic tradition of Anglo-Saxon England, "being nailed to the cross of our order." The making of vows is the profession of our willingness to be nailed onto the cross of the monastic order in the church, nailed up so that we won't get down off it.

Three nails for the cross, three vows for nailing down a man in the setting and the life to which God has called him from wandering. The nail of poverty, which pins him to community life where he has no personal property or private domain or individual autonomy, where all is shared. The nail of celibacy, which fixes the channel of his own desire, his attachment, his loving, to Christ, making it available to the Lord to transfigure and use for our good and the good of all the church. The nail of obedience, which fastens him into the enterprise of shared discernment in which the individual will is fitted to the needs and intentions of the whole body. Three nails, three hammer blows, three vows for abiding in Christ.

"I will fasten him like a peg in a secure place." This word says more than the grace of being fastened by God in the life to which God has called us. In the oracle God says he is like a carpenter who knows how to build. He knows that if the peg is to bear its weight it must go into a secure place. The trick in building is that the peg must be held in place, and by being held it actually helps everything become firmer. This image, of course, derives even greater authority from the fact that when the eternal Word of God became human, a carpenter and builder is just what it became.

The peg held in place is a good image for profession in initial vows, because it stresses the responsibility the community has for being the secure place into which a man is being fastened. I looked up the Latin text with which St. Virilar would have been familiar, *et figam illam paxillum in loco fideli. Locus fidelis*, a faithful place. When a novice brother professes his vows in a community, it is also an occasion for the whole community to make a profession. We make the profession of our fidelity, our faithfulness. We are promising to be for him a secure place that provides a sure and firm grip for his life in Christ.

Here is a mystery. As a community we are called to be the secure place into which Brian's life is driven home by the hammer blows of God. But it is this new peg that is in turn making us all firmer, more solid, more faithful. Today we become able to bear more weight, we are more secure against the elements, more solid a house of worship and hospitality. If God is still willing three years from now, we will all be gathering again for the divine carpenter to give three final strokes of the hammer. And then Brian will be in for good.

Three Wishes

The profession of initial vows of Todd Miller, SSJE, during Eastertide, at the monastery

T he official language police are always trying to limit the adoption of foreign words into French, but their success is very limited. I love the word *folklorique* from the English word "folklore." The French always use it to describe some occasion that reminds them of legend, fairy-story, and ancient customs. Today's ceremony is pretty folkloric when you think about it, and you don't have to be Joseph Campbell to describe it all in terms of legend. Let me show you.

Thirty and three moons have waxed and waned since our hero Todd cycled for forty days and forty nights from the middle of the western lands to join the band that lives on the eastern shore. Now in their shrine of stone by the river, he stands surrounded by the hero band at the moment of decision. The dim cavern is lit by a huge solitary candle. A great urn of standing water is in the center. Appearing in a cloud of scented smoke, the leader of the band, robed in an embroidered mantle, looms up and asks our hero what he wants. Now the laws of folklore positively dictate that he is going to ask for—what? Of course, he is going to ask for three wishes!

Legend tells us that asking and getting three wishes is a risky business. Story after story recounts that the hero doesn't quite realize what he is asking for, that wishes, once fulfilled, do not turn out as the hero expected. All sorts of unforeseen consequences follow. So, you see, the vows of poverty, celibacy, and obedience follow the mythic patterns of fairytale. Here is a young man on a quest who is about to make three fateful wishes whose consequences he cannot really foresee.

"Wishes!" you might be protesting. "Surely the vows of religious life are more than wishes!" Well, that is true. But they are more like the three wishes of legend than they are like a legal contract, for no real legal sanctions will bind Todd. He can always walk away from us. The vows are more like three wishes because they try to express what a man who has received this call really wants. They are expressions of committed desire. They reveal the tensions he wants to live with, the direction he wants to go, the ring he wants to wrestle in, the prizes he wants to win, the fire he wants to light, the place he wants to dwell. They are expressions of desire toward God, expressions of desire in Christ and for the kingdom.

As it happens, the font of holy water that we put in the church during the Great Fifty Days of Easter to recall the power of our baptism into Christ is the very thing we need to understand what these three wishes are really wishing for, what these vows are vowing. The font represents life itself, real life that is lived in union with God. The three wishes are expressions of three choices to enter into that true life.

Have you ever asked yourself why people throw coins into wells and fountains? I was pondering this last September when I visited the abbey of Silos in northern Spain. Outside the monastery wall there is a huge cistern of spring water that feeds into the old village washing place. The bottom was, of course, covered in coins. Even the fountains in Chinese restaurants get a constant tribute of coins, to say nothing of the fountains of Rome. Why do people throw money in pools and make a wish? The laws of legend and folklore tell us that mysterious powers dwell in deep water. Throwing money into the depths is placating those powers, buying them off, paying tribute to them to avert any danger they might pose. Although they don't know this consciously, people who throw money into pools are symbolizing their refusal to enter the depths and encounter the mysteries that lurk there. The money is a substitute for themselves. They throw in the money so that they don't have to go down into the water themselves.

The vow of poverty is a pledge to abandon the use of money as a substitute. It is a promise to dive down into the depths of life to find the mystery itself and grapple with the power that dwells there. No throwing money at life, no acquiring of things or experiences as substitutes for the pearl of great price, the "one thing necessary" that Jesus talked of, the kingdom of God and its righteousness. The vow of poverty is a promise to receive from the Spirit in the depths that unique name and identity in Christ which has nothing to do with one's wealth, income, prowess, or rank as the world weighs these things. This is the first of our hero's three wishes. Todd wants what money can't buy, and what not having money can't buy, either. Todd wants God. Poverty is the code word for that open place cleared by renunciation where God has room to appear.

The second theme that the standing water in our Easter font proclaims is simply that human beings have been created thirsty. It demands that we deal with our thirst and asks us how we intend to deal with it. Our thirst is a metaphor for deep desire, a desire to be found desirable and a desire to find someone to desire, someone eminently and completely desirable. It is this desire that sexuality expresses without exhausting it. Finding a human partner, a spouse to love, does bring fulfillment and yet still leaves more room for another level of union and encounter, desire still to be fulfilled.

In the vow of celibacy, we embrace our desire. We acknowledge that sexual partnership, if that had been our calling, would have brought fulfillment, but not ultimate fulfillment. As it is, we have been called to desire God and to discover that God desires us, and in the human unfulfillment of celibacy to allow fulfillment in the Spirit, our union with God to emerge as our true life and our real goal. In the vow of celibacy we announce that we are thirsty for love, thirsty to love and be loved. We will not drug ourselves with anything to dull the thirst. We will drink directly from the spring in prayer and worship.

> The Spirit and the bride say "Come." And let everyone who hears say, "Come." And let everyone who is thirsty come. Let anyone who wishes take the water of life as a gift." (Rev. 22:17)

We will be lovers of God. On our deathbeds we will say, "I have had a great love in my life. This great love has been the axis on which everything has turned." So this is our hero's second wish. He wishes to trust God that the celibate life in community is the place where he will get to drink directly from the spring.

And the third mystery of the standing pool, our Easter font? In ancient times before mirrors were invented, and then when they were costly luxuries only for the few, standing water was the only place human beings could see their faces reflected. The myth of Narcissus tells us that it is possible to become self-enamored. In narcissism we become fixated on our own identity, capable of seeing only the reflection of ourselves whenever we look on deep waters. Here is one of the primary symbols of human existence. The pool says we can either focus our gaze on ourselves, or we can forget our reflection and gaze into life's depths, on what is swimming around there, the real and teeming life beneath the surface. And this is what the third of the three wishes of religious profession is all about, the vow of obedience.

The vow of obedience is a renunciation of that narcissism that can only see self reflected back by life, self's obstinate demands and preferences, self's whining protests and sweet dreams, self's importunate claims and winsome seductions, self's vicious projections and thin skin. The vow of obedience is a willingness to forego the reflection from the surface for life in the water. The vow of obedience is readiness to dive into the water to meet all the otherness of life, all the other lives down there with whom God has called us to form one body in Christ. The vow of obedience is the loss of self in order to discover encounter and exchange with God's others, to risk mutuality and reciprocity, to make community, to be a co-creator and collaborator.

The vow of obedience is an expression of loss of interest in one's superficial individuality, because Christ is supremely interesting as our real identity, mine and yours, the identity that binds us all together, the mysterious identity found everywhere in friend, brother, superior, sister, guest, stranger, and enemy. So the third of our hero's three wishes is a pledge to discover the mystery of the mind of Christ and the body of Christ through community.

These are three powerful wishes. Too powerful to leap at with reckless abandon. If we allowed a new brother to bind himself for life by them as soon as he had completed his novitiate we would be accomplices in a premature decision that had not reckoned with the implications of lifelong commitment. So today, with a reverence for the intensity and risk of the quest and with a realism not always found in folktales, we allow Todd to bind himself by the vows, to apprentice himself in the quest, to make his three wishes for an initial period of three years. And then we shall gather, if all goes well, when he makes them again for good.

Do This

A requiem eucharist for Bishop David Johnson,
at the monastery, January 17, 1995

C hristianity gives us much to think about, much to figure out, and much to contemplate, but above all it gives us actions to do. Jesus, who in the agony of his last night handed himself over once and for all to us, gave us an *action* as his living legacy. "Do this in remembrance of me." So when we are in too much pain to think, too confused by grief and shock to figure anything out, and in too much turmoil to contemplate, we have something to *do*. In this awful time of shock and numbness over the death of Bishop David, death at his own hand, we are not at a loss. We do the eucharistic offering.

What are we doing? Paul tells us we are "showing forth the Lord's death until his coming again." What we have to do is to put at the center of everything we are going through the crux of it all, the cross on which God revealed his passion for us. The Lamb of God keeps us company in the worst that can befall us, suffers with us, follows us down into hell to take hold of us.

Suddenly tragedy catches us up. We had forgotten that the gospel is not about justice but about mercy, about compassion, about our redemption from the grip of death and self-destruction. Now, this evening, we show forth the Lord's death and we remember that this is all about *atonement*. We need atonement, we need redemption, and we need the blood shed for the remission of sins. All these awesome and archaic phrases we had so easily let slip into the back of our minds suddenly come to the fore. We are told to lift up the chalice of Christ's blood. Just do it!

Again, what are we doing? In the eucharist we do the act of sacrifice, of offering. We take everything we are and everything we have, we take everything Christ is and everything Christ did, and we hand it all over to God at the altar as one single offering. Today it means that we take all our grief, our rage, our heartbreak, our pity, our gratitude, our anxiety, our fear, our memories, our losses, our numbness, our injury, and we ball it all up together and let go of it by placing it into the hands and heart of Christ, offering him at the altar in the eucharistic sacrifice. Us and him, us and David and Christ, all one thing, we hand it all up to God in this eternal cross of sacrifice, praying, "It's all yours, God. Because Christ is yours, we are yours and David is yours." In the eucharist we hand ourselves over to Christ, we hand Bishop David over to Christ, and Christ hands himself over, with us bound up in him, to the undefeated love of the Father.

Again, what are we doing? We are receiving. The sad, sad death that is searing our consciousness forces us to be aware of just how needy we are, how precarious is our hold on the love and mercy of God, how fragile our hope is, how vulnerable we are. "Often were they wounded in the deadly strife" is a line in the hymn we will be singing during communion, a great hymn that meditates on our connectedness with the dead in the eucharist. It is a deadly strife, not a game. Evil is abroad, intent on trying to twist us into despair. We *need* the grace of communion; it is not an option. We need to feed on Christ, drink his life into ourselves. Now, in the emptiness of grief, our hunger and thirst come back to life in us. Feed on him in your hearts, bring your need, be poor here, open your hands.

Again, what are we doing? We are sharing. "Do this," we were told, and we are doing it *together* as we were told. Death seems to separate, grief to isolate, and suicide to flaunt before us the horror of loneliness. Christ at the very table of his betrayal and abandonment gives us the eucharist, the holy communion, so that we can do something to experience the mystery that in actuality, in reality we are all one, we are all interconnected, we are all members of a single body, breathing the same breath. We are not alone or separate, because Christ in a single day on a cross, in just two nights in the tomb, and early one Sunday morning bound us altogether forever in one, in himself. David and the Christ who saved him, ourselves and the Christ who saved us, all those who have gone before us whom Christ saved, all one, all held together in mercy.

Plumbline

One Will Be Taken

The First Sunday of Advent,
at the Church of St. Luke, Montclair, New Jersey

J esus never hesitated to use images that touch tender nerve centers in the heart. I think we will find there are at least three sore points he touches in today's gospel with these words:

> Then two will be in the field; one will be taken and one will be left. Two women will be grinding meal together; one will be taken and one will be left. (Matt. 24:40-41)

First, he probes that sensitive place inside where our fear of abandonment is lodged. No one passes through childhood without those terrible incidents where we became separated from our parents. Suddenly we looked up in the crowded shop, or on the beach, and realized that we had lost sight of them. Jesus' words, "one will be taken and one will be left," send a current through the wiring of deep insecurity left by these experiences. He speaks of a mysterious judgment that will take place at the coming of the Son of Man. It happens swiftly and silently without warning, dividing people, separating them. Some are taken up and others suddenly find themselves left behind, alone and bereft.

His words also probe the sore place of our habitual denial of death. It is almost universal for couples to say when they refer to their death, "We just hope we will both go together—we don't know what we would do without each other." But of course in real life this almost never happens. Half of us will experience the bitterness of surviving our partners. One is taken and one is left.

And the third place is our fear of being taken by surprise. Surprise presents and surprise parties are one thing, but most of us like warnings to prepare us for everything else. Jesus unnerves us by telling us that God's judgment has no build up, no series of preparatory signs and stages. Life goes on exactly as it always has. Food is being prepared. Two women are in the kitchen. Careers are being pursued. Two men will be in the field, or in the office. Life for the most part centers on the family. People, as Jesus says, are marrying and giving in marriage. Food, work, sex, companionship, home, children—even liquor is mentioned, for Jesus liked life and liked wine enough to have been accused of being a lush by his enemies. "For as in those days before the flood they were eating and drinking"—liquor has long taken the edge off life's pain and blurred the difficulties of staying in love with one's partner. But just as the whole population was taken by complete surprise when the flood came, so, warns Jesus, we run the risk of being taken completely unaware by the judgment of God.

Now although Jesus is using mythical language, the dramatic idiom of judgment the scholars call apocalyptic, the picture he paints is curiously and disturbingly simple and bare. All he says is that the judgment of God takes place in the context of perfectly normal life. If God at any time should stop time in its tracks and take home to himself those who are ready for union with him and desire his presence, then what would happen? "Two will be in the field; one will be taken and one will be left. Two women will be grinding meal together; one will be taken and one will be left." Judgment consists in the exposure of something that has been true all along but hidden—that some of us desire intimacy with God and are entering into it now, in daily life, ready to let that intimacy come to fullness when death finally sets us free for it, and some of us are not really interested in intimacy with God. Some of us want God at a safe distance, or we are so spiritually asleep as to be unaware of even the possibility of being in love with God, and of God being in love with us.

Judgment is presented here not as a matter of wickedness and innocence. There are two in the field; there is no suggestion that the one taken is a saint and the one left is evil. What makes the difference is awareness. The one left behind was unaware and unprepared for something that the one who is taken knew about and was ready for. St. Matthew stresses that this whole discourse of Jesus was delivered in private to the disciples, not to a mixed crowd of worldly people; Jesus is not talking about "other people." What Jesus said to the disciples he says to us as a church of worshiping and believing people: we run the risk of being unaware and unready for what God is preparing for us. If we remain in our ignorance and lack of readiness, we will exclude ourselves.

The key questions, then, are: "What is God preparing for us?" and "How do we show that we are getting ready for it?" Heaven won't do as an answer to the first question. We have to say what heaven is. Heaven is union with God. "Father, I desire that those also, whom you have given me, may be with me where I am, to see my glory" (John 17:24). Heaven is being united with Christ and joined with him in love to the Creator, receiving from the Father limitless love and the fullness of his Spirit. Heaven is our becoming ourselves divine through intimacy with God, "participants of the divine nature," as the second letter of Peter puts it.

"How do we show that we are getting ready for it?" If heaven is the consummation of intimacy with God, then there is only one way we could show we wanted to get ready for that—by practicing the first steps of intimacy with God in the midst of our daily lives. Prayer is what we do to practice the first steps of intimacy. In prayer we get out of the habit of concealing our feelings from God; we express our desires, our needs, our frustrations, our regrets, our caring for others, our doubts. In prayer we open ourselves to what God is saying to us by reading Scripture and allowing it to touch our lives. In prayer we look over our lives for signs of God's grace and activity, offering him our appreciation when we find them and our frustration when we can't. We open our eyes to what is happening in the world and question God about it, growing in honesty and trying to incorporate the values of the Beatitudes into our way of looking at life. If you pray, you show that you are getting ready for intimacy with God. You may not pray well, but you are practicing the scales of intimacy, and in God's future you will come into your own.

If you do not pray, then the warning light is on. Are you avoiding intimacy with God? If you are, there will probably be other signs, too. Addictions are primary signs, especially addiction to overwork and overcommitment, or to alcohol. Addictions tend to make us impotent in all forms of intimacy, intimacy with partners and children as well as intimacy with God, and thus they serve to close off that whole area we want to avoid. Another sign is rationalizations that insist prayer is for the birds, or doesn't work, or is too time-consuming. There will be unspoken assumptions that church membership, or all the work you do for the church, will see you through. There will be a bias toward the pragmatic, and a slight scorn for spirituality as marginal, mystical, and effeminate.

The biblical image for that state of denial, the deliberate shutting down of the spiritual life, the flight from intimacy and awareness, is sleep. It is the sleep of a bad hangover, full of illusions and self-hatred. To break the denial and start enjoying a personal communion with God is like waking up to the joys and pains of awareness, alertness, and sobriety. Numbness wears off, dreams fade, and you are in daylight, for "you know what time it is, how it is now the moment for you to wake from sleep" (Rom. 13:11).

"Watch, stay awake!" are words we know to have been constantly on Jesus' lips. At the beginning of every new liturgical year it gives us the clue to Christ's will for this community and every church. He wants this to be a community that cultivates alertness and awareness of God in everyday life. He wants it to be a community that knows how to call its people on the rationalizations they use to mask their avoidance of God. He wants it to be a school of intimacy with God, a place where we can be healed of the preoccupied states of mind that make us numb and impotent. He wants it to be a community where we can learn how to stay in touch with God and one another, with eyes and hearts open and awake.

Coming Out
to Meet Him

The Season after Pentecost,
at the Church of the Holy Comforter, Kenilworth, Illinois

Perhaps Jesus' strange story in the twenty-fifth chapter of Matthew's gospel about the behavior of a group of bridesmaids at a village wedding has more to tell us about what it is to be a church than dozens of diocesan reports about mission and renewal. Perhaps it is part of God's sense of humor to hide his challenges and promises in ironic parables, while keeping his distance from our serious religious projects.

If we let it speak to us, the challenges of this parable come thick and fast. The kingdom of heaven will be like a big wedding reception. Stop there! God's sovereignty is like a big party—celebration, festivity, conviviality. You might ask yourself right away whether visitors or newcomers to your church would get that impression from its worship, teaching, and parish life. Jesus kept on talking about banquets and invitations and festivities, and went to a lot of them himself. Some people got the point and others didn't. God is here with us to be enjoyed. The mission of the church is to be a community within which people receive their invitation to enter into the joy of God. We aren't the ones issuing the invitation; God does the inviting. But we can be the setting in which that invitation is heard by people who haven't heard it before. We can be a community within which it dawns on people that God actually invites us.

The gospels record that Jesus went to a lot of parties in the homes of racketeering taxgatherers and prostitutes who found him and his message attractive. There couldn't be a clearer way of saying that the invitation of God is extended to all. When we issue invitations to our parties, we make them exclusive affairs. We gather the like-minded, "our kind of people." The God of Jesus is sheer holiness and yet when it comes to love he is, well, kind of promiscuous. Everyone gets asked. You will remember the story Jesus told about the man who is throwing a wedding party and gets all sorts of polite refusals at the last minute. He orders his staff to comb the hedgerows and back streets to round up anyone and everyone for the celebration.

All this puts our parish life to some pretty severe tests. Does this community convey to all comers that there is a place for them at the table of God, that they belong in the body of Christ, that something is lacking in the celebration unless they join in? Or do you convey all sorts of coded messages to certain people that they wouldn't fit in and had better look elsewhere?

And what about bridesmaids? What do bridesmaids do? I was thinking about that a couple of months ago when I was in a lakeside park in Canada on my retreat day. On Saturday dozens of wedding parties appeared out of nowhere and posed endlessly for the camera all day against the background of the flowers and the waves. What were those bridesmaids there for? They didn't really do anything. They were there simply to be attractive! They were there as a foil for the bride and groom, to create a splash of colorful splendor as a setting for them. In Jesus' day the bridesmaids' big moment came in the evening, when they lit the bridegroom's way down the street into the house, forming a resplendent escort. Surrounded by lovely young women with twinkling lamps, the groom made his grand entrance.

Matthew sets the story out as an allegory of the second coming of Christ. Christ will be shown forth in glory accompanied by those faithful disciples who have been watchful and resourceful. On the other hand, disciples who were distracted and careless will find themselves left behind and shut out of the celebration. They have missed what is essential in discipleship, that expectant focus on the bridegroom.

The kick in the story is that the church has a lot of people in it who haven't grasped their role and are missing the point of the whole enterprise. When the moment for action arrives, they can't function. When a church takes stock to see whether it has got what it takes to be a gospel community, constantly extending an invitation into the joy of God, there comes a moment of truth. What do we do when the moment for action arrives? Do some of us suddenly find ourselves confused and ill-equipped, unable to join in, left groping around when others take off?

So we ask ourselves again, what is the role of the bridesmaid? At the right time she is to step out into the dark to meet the bridegroom, to keep him company, to draw attention to his arrival at the house, to use her lamp to focus everyone's attention on his presence at the party. That is the role of the informed and converted disciple, too. Our role is to step out to meet Christ in person, to keep him company, to announce his arrival, to draw everyone's attention to his presence. It is an image of the disciple as evangelist. The disciple evangelist goes out to meet Christ, stays close to him, sheds light on the moments of his arrival in life so that others may greet and know him, draws the attention of all to Christ's risen presence among us as the heart and focus of our celebration of God's mercy and love.

Let's concentrate on the moment of truth at the heart of the parable:

But at midnight there was a shout, "Look! Here is the bridegroom! Come out to meet him!" (Matt. 25:6)

I have always found this to be one of the key sentences in the entire New Testament. It seems to sum up Christian spirituality in a single invitation: "Here is the bridegroom!" It is not "Here is the moral example!" "Here is the arbiter of good ethics!" "Here is the teacher!" Christ is the embodiment of God's being in love with us. Christ is the lover and bridegroom of our hearts and souls. Real life with Christ begins when we allow ourselves to meet him as the one who loves. Too many of us in Christian congregations never have.

"Come out to meet him!" There can never be any real meeting with Christ unless we are prepared to come out. To meet Christ we have to leave what is safe and familiar. Take the business of prayer, for example. Most of us are educated to value externals; we are wedded to facts and to the familiar territory of everyday routines. But prayer opens up into mystery, where beneath the level of appearances God can be sensed in the heart, and Christ can be spoken to, loved, desired, thanked, and heard within. For the hardboiled, "just the facts, ma'am," types that most of us were trained to be, prayer is impossible unless we come out into the mysterious realm of the Spirit who searches our depths.

I find the words about the cry going up at midnight especially poignant. I will never forget the first retreat I gave for priests, where I decided to base the whole retreat on this text of scripture. I talked about the night, about the presence of darkness in our lives, about how Christ often comes to us when it is dark. I hardly knew what I was saying, but at once every retreatant signed up to talk to me and each one needed to talk about the real darkness in their lives, about barrenness and fear, about addiction and shame, about grief. I was taken aback by the suffering I saw within them. Now I know better about how people fight to hide their suffering, and how much they need Christ to come to them in the night.

Christian spirituality and Christian evangelism are based on a fundamental honesty about the presence of darkness in our lives. Both fight the denial of death and the stupid, feel-good rhetoric that superficial religion uses to drive suffering under-ground. Faith that is true to the gospel of the cross and resur-rection says to suffering human beings, "It *is* dark. But through the darkness Christ the lover is approaching. Come out into the night. You will meet him there, coming to you."

The renewal of a church for mission hasn't much to do with elaborate training programs for getting new members into the net. Renewal comes when, to borrow a phrase from the scien-tists, a "critical mass" of disciples have the courage to leave a safe level of conventional religion and go out to meet Christ and come to know him for themselves. They come to name him and love him. They become able to shed light for others on his presence. To come out to meet him, they have to make room in their lives for prayer and inner work that faces the re-ality of death, darkness, and denial in their lives. To come out to meet him they have to sacrifice pastimes, activities, and time-fillers so that their encounter with him can be central, not peripheral, to their lives.

So You Want to Get Rid of Sin?

Lent, at the monastery

T he French novelist Julien Green was born of American
parents who had emigrated after the defeat of the South
in the Civil War. Recently I have been reading his journals,
and all sorts of odd and thought-provoking questions from
them remain in my mind. Above all there are two sharp sentences:

> *"Je veux chasser le péché de chez moi," dit le chrétien. "C'est
> ça," fait l'orgeuil, "et je vais t'y aider. Comme ça nous serons
> tranquille."*

> "I want to get rid of sin from my life," says the Christian.
> "That's right," says Pride, "and I'm going to help you. That
> way things will be peaceful for both of us."

Once read, that kind of insight remains like a barb in the
brain that from time to time will prick us into awareness that
our moods of moral fervor and desire to be good are not always what they seem to be. They can be the most dangerous
of temptations. Deep down pride may be reaching out after an
illusory condition of superiority and invulnerability. Wouldn't it

be wonderful never to need to ask for anyone's forgiveness? Wouldn't it be good not to trip up? Wouldn't it be gratifying to be admired as a good person—while having, of course, the humility to take it all in one's stride? Wouldn't it be good (of course, we can't allow this to become fully conscious!) to be better than others? Purely in order to be of help, you understand.

Corruptio optimi pessima, the Latin tag goes. "The worst thing is the best gone bad." Jesus was fiercely conscious of the demonic possibilities in the desire to be perfect; that is the explanation of his unrelenting criticism of the Pharisees, most of whom were devout people of passionate moral seriousness. It makes the religious life a dangerous business; inside every religious vocation is a can of worms. One particularly slippery one at the bottom is the craving to be spiritually above the crowd. It makes you wonder whether God simply refuses to take the risk of giving us holiness on these terms. Perhaps it is better for the kingdom of God that we should keep tripping up rather than settle down in peace with our helpful partner Pride after sin has been put out the door.

Perhaps it would be useful to play with this idea that crops up constantly in the writings of spiritual teachers, and to ask, "Is there a pattern of divine training to be discerned in our ongoing struggle with sin? Is there moral and spiritual meaning behind the fact that we go on being susceptible to sin? Can grace actually exploit our persistent frailties to *bring about that dependence* on him that God so prizes?

There is precious little warrant in Christian tradition for the notion that perfection is a condition of achieved invulnerability, a safe state of not sinning. As in the gospels, perfection consists rather in humility and compassion for others. "Those who see themselves as they truly are and have seen their sin are greater than those who raise the dead" is a typical saying of St. Isaac the Syrian; another is "Purity of heart is love for those who fall."

So we can start off by saying that God, in refusing to wave a magic wand to make us perfect overnight, and in leaving us in our susceptibility to faults and failings, is putting us into a school of humility and patience. We are so keen to correct and improve others, so sure that they could be better if only they pulled themselves together! Then we are left to experience in our own case just how hard it is to change and grow in order that we may learn to be patient with ourselves. God withholds any artificial protection or premature changes that would disguise our common human neediness and moral poverty. He forces us to recognize, in Jung's words, "that the least among them all, the poorest of all the beggars, the most impudent of all the offenders, the very enemy himself, that these are within me and that I myself am the enemy who must be loved." When at length we gain the maturity of that acceptance and are enabled to share it with others, then perhaps the path is clear for God in his own good time to clear up some of our besetting sins.

The mention of God's good time raises the other aspect of the word patience, the temporal aspect. God mustn't know whether to laugh or cry over the naiveté and impatience that underlie the new convert's surprise that old sins aren't weeded out in a month and that all sorts of objectionable struggles and backslidings appear in no time on the scene. The work of conversion is a process of organic growth, not a conjuring trick. St. Paul speaks of *Christ being formed* in us. This formation has as many stages as Christ's formation in Mary's womb and through his thirty years in Nazareth. We have stages to go through, experiences to undergo, sufferings to pass through before certain wounds can be healed or habits outgrown.

Significant among these converting experiences are our personal relationships; we need others to help us grow and change. Perhaps years have to pass before providence brings us into contact with someone through whose example and love God can heal us of some defect. We must take our time—that is the burden of countless classic spiritual letters. Or rather, we must learn that God takes his time, that his action in our lives has its own pace and cadence, and his priorities may be radically different from ours. It takes most of us an awfully long time before we begin to get the message.

According to the great spiritual teachers, our repeated falls can actually be instrumental in deepening and cementing our relationship with God. An enormous amount hangs on how resilient we are when we fall. We can either become cynical and discouraged, or we can rage at ourselves, picking off the scabs in regret and nursing feelings of shame and hurt pride in self-prolonging orgies of guilt. This latter reaction is unanimously regarded as a triumph for the Evil One, far more destructive than the sinning itself. De Caussade writes in *Abandonment to Divine Providence:*

> Fear, especially if carried to excess after whatever fault you have committed, proceeds from the devil. Instead of giving in to this dangerous illusion, use every effort to repulse it and cast uneasiness away as you would cast a stone into the sea and never dwell upon it voluntarily. This applies equally to that feeling of uneasiness and distress which proceeds from constant little infidelities. This oppression of the heart is also occasioned by the devil.

Instead, the saints teach us a daring elasticity, a loving resilience that keeps us getting up again and setting our sights on the will of God, keeps us rededicating ourselves in trust and renewed dependence over and over again.

It is beautifully put by a sixteenth-century Italian spiritual writer, Lorenzo Scupoli, in his manual *Spiritual Combat*. He advises the penitent, after turning to God for forgiveness and mercy:

> Do not torment yourself with thoughts as to whether God has forgiven you. The Lord is near and listens to the sighings of His servants. So calm yourself in this certainty...and continue

your usual occupations as though nothing had happened. You must do this not once but, if necessary, a hundred times and every minute, and the last time with the same perfect trust and daring toward God as the first.

Finally, consider how important it is for God to make sure that many of our best-meant efforts to reform ourselves by resolutions, will power, and good intentions come to nothing, and how much many of us need disillusioning in this regard. We want to do it *ourselves*. Actually God doesn't have to do very much for these efforts to come to nothing—except to step aside. Most of our own self-conscious efforts to do better are futile because they are superficial treatments of symptoms, not causes.

St. Paul has a phrase for it: "the mystery of iniquity." Iniquity is a baffling mystery on a cosmic scale. How did evil arise? And it is a mystery in each one of us—why we do what we do—only fully known by God. But it is almost useless to try to suppress the external symptoms if the deep interior causes are not faced and explored. Beneath the upper levels of psychological cause and effect, our faith holds that at root our sins are gambits, substitutes, games, and compensations, a thousand manifestations of an unsatisfied hunger for the living God. We lack God so we treat ourselves as our creator, or make others into our gods, and the result is a myriad of destructive games. We lack the all-surpassing divine love which is Father, Son, and Holy Spirit and alone can meet our craving, so we clutch at *ersatz* satisfactions and try to wring from others what their maker alone can give.

Only sinking into God can change us from within. This means that conversion, far from consisting of self-control, is essentially self-surrender, self-abandonment, worship. The changes that no resolutions of the ego can achieve take place secretly behind our backs and in the hidden springs of the heart while we are learning to look to God and trust him absolutely with our life in Christ Jesus.

The Night

August, at the monastery

"I have been thinking these past days," the novelist Julien Green once wrote in his diary, "about Jesus singing. He sang with the apostles on Maundy Thursday before going to his death. What kind of voice did he have? And also he must have dreamed while he slept. The gospels mention his sleeping more than once. What did he dream?"[1]

This thought intrigues me. Have you ever imagined Jesus dreaming? Most people find this train of thought quite threatening to pursue. We don't find it easy to face the real humanity of Jesus, do we? We all know what our dreams are like, with their weird violence, their surrealist dramas, their kaleidoscope of sexual experience. If this is human dreaming, what was Jesus' human dreaming like? Jesus never wavered from truth and obedience, but he was tempted in every way as we are, so what about the unconscious life of his nights?

We can't pretend to know, but perhaps the question about Jesus' experience of the night rebounds on us. Our human sleeping and dreaming have been shared by the Son of God, so it may be that we should go on asking ourselves, what does this part of life mean? Perhaps God is still our God while we are asleep, and he can be for us and touch us in our nights. Our sleeping and dreaming can be understood as religious experience. What we know of the Lord can lead us to the deep roots of this activity—or do I mean inactivity?—that takes up a third of our time on earth.

Earlier in this diary, Green tells a little story about a friend from La Rochelle.

> The lady has a colossal Great Dane who adores his mistress. His demonstrations of love are frequently so noisy that conversation in her tiny Parisian apartment becomes difficult. "Just you see," she said calmly and pulled out a revolver from her sewing basket. Clapping the gun to the dog's temple, she fires it. The dog collapses. But no harm done. It was a starting pistol. The dog gets the message and goes to sleep.[2]

I love it! A parable! It is as if through sleep God has found a trick to compel us to stop the furor of our activity, to halt the momentum of our interfering with one another, to sabctage our overcontrol and suspend our drivenness. We are so capable, we have so much to do, but inexorably and inevitably we fall down into silence and none can hold out against the invisible opium for very long. Sleep is a constant visitor sent from God to give us the same message every evening. "Now you have to surrender your control, surrender your consciousness, surrender your creativity."

How do we treat this familiar angel? Some treat her with rage and resistance, those who are consumed by the need to preserve mastery through activity. They fall into a fitful sleep with bad grace and anxiety. There are others who seem unable to let this angel in at all, terrified of the surrender. How many tons of soporific drugs do the pharmaceutical factories churn out to meet the demand of anxious millions who need to be overpowered into sleep?

I suppose the faithful give this angel a welcome, if at times a rueful one. The faithful believe in the intrinsic rightness of rest. They trust the solitude, the space and respite it gives in our relationships with one another. (An old speculation was that Adam was taught how to sleep before Eve appeared—so that he would give her eight hours of peace out of the twenty-four!) The faithful also consent to sleep as a basic recognition that we are not the Creator, God is. The world will still be there when we wake because it is God who holds it in life.

Sleep is a nightly rehearsal for the arrival of the last messenger, the angel of death, who will call us to an absolute letting-go in trust. Julien Green was one of the great interpreters of the writings of Charles Péguy, who spoke so wonderfully of night and surrender in his poem, "The Mystery of the Holy Innocents":

But the man who calculates, for tomorrow,
   who inwardly in his head
Works like a mercenary,
Works horribly like a slave turning an eternal wheel,
(And between ourselves like a fool)
Well, he doesn't please me at all, God says.
The man who abandons himself, I love.
The man who doesn't abandon himself, I do not love....

It is then, O night, that you come.
And what you did once upon a time,
You do every time.
What you did one day,
You do every day.
As you came down one evening,
So you came down every evening.
What you did for my Son made man,
O great Charity, you do for all men, his brothers.
You shroud them in silence and shadow
And in healthy forgetfulness
Of the mortal anxiety
Of the day.
What you did once for my Son made man,
What you did one evening among all evenings,
O night, you do again every evening for the least of men.[3]

But it is not oblivion we abandon ourselves to on our beds. *Ego dormio cor meum vigilat*, "I am asleep but my heart is wide awake," says the biblical adage our ancestors knew so well. Sleep sets free rich processes in the depth of the psyche and soul, especially through dreaming. The censorship of the waking mind must be suspended before they can come to life. These processes are apparently more than merely beneficial; waking people up whenever electronic monitors show that they have entered the kind of sleep that enables dreaming proves to have a pernicious effect on their mental health.

Is God a stranger to these processes? Is he a mere alien observer of the buzzing, clicking, and flashing that goes on in the brain? Or is the Holy Spirit who brooded over the waters of chaos also the one who broods over our depths and stirs in the nightlife of the heart? Our forbearers in the faith would be amazed at our modern difficulty in giving a clear affirmative. Of course God can see and work in the dark! Of course the Spirit of Pentecost is a master of the metaphorical language system of the psyche that is so vivid, detailed, and concrete! Actually the Spirit is far more fluent in that language than in English.

How might we imagine the Spirit's work in the night? First, let us risk believing that God has a stake in our facing up to and dealing with all that comes out of the heart, because our humanity and humility and wisdom depend on it. In dreaming we are invited to come to terms with ourselves as microcosms of very vulnerable and somewhat crazy humanity. In dreams we act out our sexuality, we act out our murderousness, we suffer our fears and obsessions, and we are led along some heroic and beautiful paths. We start up from a dream, shaken by its exceptionally moving power, and our tidy, tight daytime identity is blown apart. Does not the Spirit of truth want us to allow the nightlife of the heart to "serve our enlightenment"?

If we have faith, there will be times when the signs of grace will truly be present in a dream. It may not be as fateful as the dreams of Jacob, Joseph, Peter, and Paul, but it will bring the gift of disclosure, consolation, warning, or resolution. Then we will be thankful to the Holy Spirit.

But if the Spirit does sometimes touch us with exact and timely relevance in certain special dreams, we can be sure that the whole dream life constitutes a constant message to us that we are inclined to ignore. Every night we rediscover that our native language is symbol and image. All of us are virtuosi of myth and metaphor and imagination once we lie down to sleep; this is the only language in which the deepest part of ourselves can address us. But we fail to take seriously the fact that it works the other way. The language of symbol and imagination is the language—the only effective language—in which we can address and affect and actively impregnate our deepest selves.

If the gospel is to penetrate to the very depths, and not just remain as mere concept, then we must admit it into the heart through assimilation of sacrament and image. "In the exercises of St. Ignatius," Rahner reminds us in his *Spiritual Dialogue at Evening,* "one of the essential parts of his schemes of meditation is the activation of the *vista imaginativa,* which represents the object of the meditation to the person in a great image. And this image is to be taken with one right into sleep so that it springs before the mind immediately in the morning."

There are searching questions hidden in these matters for all of us. How vividly present to your heart are the great images in which the supreme reality, God, has come near to us and impressed itself on our world? How vividly do you recollect them to yourself and feed upon them in your heart by faith with thanksgiving? How intimate and accessible to you are they through meditation on the scriptures and experience of the liturgy? Do you pray them? Or does your prayer deal in ideas and abstractions, or the perfunctory sifting of private concerns and general issues? A lot depends on the answer you give.

And at night. Do you pray before sleep? How do you pray before sleep? Is it a mere lazy signing-off? Or do you imaginatively lay hold of faith in Christ and the cross as you enter the strange world of the night with the blessing of his holy company, and his power over chaos and death?

Notes

1. Julien Green, *Vers L'Invisible* (Paris: Plon, 1967), 424.
2. Ibid., 121.
3. Charles Péguy, *The Mystery of the Holy Innocents & Other Poems,* trans. Pansy Pakenham (London: The Harvill Press, 1956), 79.

Wash and Be Clean

Next week is Shrove Tuesday, the traditional day for confession, so maybe my theme is predictable. I had almost decided to take another subject altogether when I had a dream. In the dream I was in my garden, which was very densely planted, trying to find a place to put a rambler rose. After much searching for a space I found only one that was suitable, against the wire fence of my neighbor at the back. Just on the other side an old man, bald, toothless, and tattooed, sat half-buried in the dirt, mumbling in confusion and discomfort. My first reaction was to withdraw and try a find another place to plant my rose, but this was the only place.

The miserable old man grew quieter, now almost completely buried in the dirt. I knew what I had to do. I put my rose down and went round to the little house and spoke to the mother and her little daughter who came to the door. "The old man, he needs pulling out and washing and caring for," I said. Without any upset or fuss, the three of us calmly went down to the fence and pulled him gently to his feet. He seemed so relieved to be taken into the house by the woman and the little girl. I left him in their care and went back onto my side of the fence, where I could then plant the rose bush.

I have no claims whatever to be an interpreter of dreams, but this one had a parable-like quality. I think I am like many people who are genuinely searching for space to let something new grow in their lives. When it comes to working on that place I don't like to be faced with the sight of a human being who is powerless, filthy, and ruined. I don't want to think that the place of new life makes me reckon with this alter ego. So I turn away, hoping that the real place for newness lies elsewhere, in a more wholesome and sheltered place in the garden. But evasion won't work. I return to the spot and realize that the wretched one is slipping out of sight through my neglect and if I continue to look away he might go underground, beyond my reach. Then there would be no way I would dare do any planting there. The alternative is to offer some comfort to the soiled and confused old man who is also me, and needs to be lifted up and brought back into the house to be washed and attended to. When that is being done I can then attend to the new thing I want to cultivate in my life.

Put more simply, it doesn't do us any good to ignore the damaged, recalcitrant, and soiled selves within us. Neglected, they go underground and, decomposing out of sight, spoil our growth. Our sinful self needs care. If we give care to our sinful self, we have room for new growth in our lives. The church's sacramental ministry of reconciliation is a means whereby the community helps us care for the sinful self so that we can keep on growing.

If you like a touch of allegory in the dream, the mother and the child who take the dirty old man inside to be washed again and tended could be the church. There is no scene, no great drama. Love takes him in, and in counsel and absolution simply and straightforwardly does what is needed. He will be back out there in the dirt, acting out crazily in some way or other before too long, but so what? We will bring him in and run the bathwater again just as before, and do what needs to be done. And the ministers of the church are ready for the repeat performance of forgiveness just like the women in the dream.

A couple of questions, then. First, are you able to name sin and the sins in your own life? If you are and do, well and good. But don't imagine this ability is all that common, even among regular worshipers. It takes imagination and courage to look at yourself and say, "I grieve the Holy Spirit, I block the action of God in my life, I act out of mistrust and fear, I treat others as though they were worthless." It takes work and insight and prayer to go on to say, "And this is how I do it," telling the story of how and when and where and to whom, concretely. It isn't all that easy to be as specific and factual in our own personal prayer to God, to say nothing of the prayers of confession in the liturgy.

Yet the integrity of true forgiveness depends on this concreteness, this naming of the acts of the sinful self. Never was the adage "Truth is concrete" truer than it is here. Generalized blaming, diffuse guilt, all-embracing formulas of self-disparagement are useless. Our sins are recognizable patterns as particular as the tattoos that marked the body of the old man in my dream. Scenes of neglect and hurt have our particular fingerprints all over them.

In the church's sacrament of reconciliation we are helped to break out of our inveterate habit of vagueness that insulates us from the real experience of forgiveness in Christ. In sacramental confession we can't get away with it. We have to present our sinful selves intelligibly to a brother or sister. We have to name our God-resisting behavior with names that make sense to the Christian community he or she represents. In confession I won't try and get away with private psychologizing and complicated excuses; I know I am there just to tell the story and talk straight.

Second question. Do you experience forgiveness, the loving contact between God in Christ and the sinful self? Do you experience God embracing you as a sinner? Is the joy of letting go and being given a fresh start in intimacy with God an experience you can identify in your life?

If the answer is yes, well and good. But for many, forgiveness is not so much an experience as an idea. We think of our faults and we think of God as forgiving, but then there is a break in the circuit—no current, no spark, no power. There is a world of difference between believing that God is forgiving and actually allowing Christ to get down and wash your feet. Instead we indulge in introspection, sending our intellects out like ferrets to search for the hidden causes of our behavior, paralyzing ourselves with questions about responsibility and free will, prolonging our self-fascination. It flies in the face of the tradition that warns us not to let sin suck us into self-absorption but instead turn simply and resolutely toward the accepting Father who desires to embrace and heal us, not to dismantle and reprogram us. What our sinful selves need are not intellectual solutions but love and the washing of wounds and the clothing of shame.

This is just what is offered in the sacrament of reconciliation. People hesitate to approach sacramental confession because they fear intellectual disappointment: "The advice won't be subtle enough. The whole things sounds dangerously simpleminded, too straightforward. How can something so conventional deal with the complexity of my own condition?" This attitude reminds me of Naaman the Syrian, who was incensed at Elisha's very routine-sounding prescription to bathe seven times in the Jordan in order to cure his leprosy. Naaman was sure that something far more sophisticated was called for and it took some level-headed servants to persuade him to try it, simple as it was.

Come to think of it, those servants are people I can really identify with. The church at this time of the year, with Lent coming up, offers the sacrament of reconciliation. No big sales pitch, no big deal, no complications or justifications. It simply says that if you want to experience forgiveness thoroughly, don't mess with your sins in your mind. Get off your high horse and join the line for confession. The simplicity of the act of confession is part of the cure. Give up being a special case and join the mob of ordinary battered mortals who mess up. Let the soiled old man in you feel the embrace of Christ in quite unambiguous words of absolution that don't leave room for argument. Listen to your priest apply the good news of the gospel to you personally. Feel the shock of Christ's unconditional love. Listen to some encouragement. Then leave everything behind with God. Send it on its way. Go away and get on with life and whenever you feel any temptation to get back into regret or guilt, say "I'm forgiven" and just move on.

It sounds simple and it is, in a way that wounds our pride. So maybe it is enough to offer you these simple words from the second book of Kings, the words of Naaman's shrewd servants.

> But his servants approached and said to him, "Father, if the prophet had commanded you to do something difficult, would you not have done it? How much more, when all he said to you was, 'Wash, and be clean'?" (2 Kings 5:13)

Passions

Love Knows
No Seasons

Tuesday in Holy Week, at the monastery

H ow much intensity of feeling can the human heart bear? We can go some way in guessing at the feelings of a soldier about to go into battle, a victim awaiting execution, a man certain that his friends are about to betray or desert him, a lover rejected, someone returning home in utter failure. But none of these begins to approach the melting point of feeling that Jesus must have experienced in the final days before his crucifixion. We can try to imagine something of his loneliness, his anguish, his desire to get through the baptism with which he was to be baptized and to plunge into the presence of his God. But we can hardly begin to sense what it meant for him to know that his rejection was the climactic repudiation of divine love, the terrible proof that humankind preferred the embrace of death and sterility to the arms of its Creator and Lover. We dare not admit into our own selves the molten stream of Jesus' self-abandonment as he threw his whole being against the tide of reaction to save us, in case the thin vessels of our own hearts should crack in the heat.

As we celebrate the Passion we must sense the heat of passion in the heart of Jesus, even though it is a furnace we cannot stand to look into directly. Everything this week is passion, from the moment Christ's heart was warmed and fortified by the woman who anointed his head with ointment in the house of Simon the leper to the agonizing struggles beneath the olive trees in Gethsemane. Today we are confronted by two blazings-out of Jesus' passion in the cursing of the fig tree and the cleansing of the temple.

It is painful to recall the sermons of English clergymen I have listened to on the cursing of the fig tree. "Here we cannot but feel that some misunderstanding, some exaggeration, has crept into the gospels," they intone. "We can hardly suppose that Jesus would commit an act so—pardon the expression!—petulant as to curse a tree for not having fruit on it when it wasn't even the season. No, no, surely the Master who contemplated the lilies of the field could hardly have stooped to cursing, et cetera." The mild-mannered preachers devoted to gardening have to part company with the evangelist when it comes to blasting an innocent tree.

Jesus is walking down from Bethany, hungry and impassioned. He is hungry but not only for food—for some response, some glimmer of assurance that his companions know what is at stake, understand what is happening. And there is the fig tree, splendid in its glossy leaves and sinuous gray branches. He goes up to it and rummages among the branches until the disciples begin to get curious about the significance of this pantomime.

"No figs!" he yells at them. "No fruit!" The disciples exchange meaningful looks. They have had these scenes before—Jesus is being irrational and provocative again. "Of course there are no figs," they patiently explain. "Figs tree don't have figs in April, remember? It isn't the season for figs." The more daring of them, out of Jesus' direct line of vision, tap the sides of their heads and roll their eyes, murmuring, "Jesus, pleeze!" But then it doesn't seem so funny when Jesus solemnly curses the tree: "May no one ever eat fruit from you again!" They don't understand because they aren't looking where Jesus is looking. Through the branches of the fig tree, across the Kidron valley, Jesus can see the temple.

The terrible thing is that Jesus condemns a living, healthy tree. It does produce fruit when the season comes round, when the time is right, but it is this very characteristic that makes it the symbol of the failure of God's people. Like the tree, the response of God's people is limited to certain seasons, certain times when conditions are just right. When the time isn't right, God mustn't expect any fruit. And it is this seasonal, fluctuating, intermittent pattern of response that Jesus has come to challenge and overthrow. It is not overt rebellion against God that Jesus condemns, but viewing the covenant as something we can live up to only part of the time, when things are going right and conditions are favorable. When the disciples say, "But you can't expect figs when it isn't the right time," they are voicing the self-justification of God's people, explaining why they couldn't rise up to the life of covenant just now.

So Jesus takes his disciples directly to the temple. The temple is very much alive, the center of national identity in an enemy-occupied land ruled by pagan Romans. Since the Gentiles have the upper hand, this is hardly the time for the temple to be God's house of prayer for all the Gentiles, as the prophets had ordained. The time is not ripe to make concessions to pagan oppressors and the swarming Gentiles from all over the empire squatting on Israel's sacred land and exploiting it. This is not the time for ecumenism, for Israel is at risk. The temple and all it represents is for Israel alone. It would be unrealistic for the Court of the Gentiles to be truly available to everyone for pilgrimage and prayer. Jews must have a market for the sacrificial animals; while theoretically this space is reserved for foreigners, in practice, taking the current political situation into account, it is the best site for the market.

Jesus bursts passionately into the temple and enacts the long-overdue reform of clearing the space needed for the temple to be God's house of prayer for all the earth's peoples. What he attacks is that resistance to God's will that takes the form of claims like, "The time is not yet ripe....It would be premature....We must wait until a more auspicious season comes round....In our present condition God can hardly expect....For the time being our interests need defending....In due season we might be able to afford...." Jesus proclaims the abolition of seasonal love, seasonal fidelity, seasonal obedience. The fruit that God seeks knows no seasons, no winter, no time of abeyance. Love has no fallow times, no hibernation. He judges those excuses of seasonal response that are the stock-in-trade of politicians, the constant refrain of ecclesiastics, and the stuff of our interior conversations by which we decide that we cannot afford at present to reach out in the love that builds a just community.

So Jesus curses the fig tree. Or to be precise, he cries out for the disciples to hear, "May no one eat fruit from you again!" It is as if he turns to us and says, "You are hungry like me but don't ever touch this stuff again. Don't accept the ideology of seasonal response. My food is to do the will of him who sent me, and to accomplish his work. If you would only recognize that this is what you hunger for, too! Your hunger will never really be satisfied unless you find the secret of constancy, a love for God that is at the ready in season and out of season."

His words appalled the disciples and they appall us. The love he is talking about has no guarantees, no safety nets; it puts everything at risk. But Jesus says no more. He acts. He acts the abandonment of security, the letting-go of all guarantees, by going to the cross. As a mere demonstration of that love it would have been magnificent, but it was more than a gesture. It released this love into the community. On the cross the rock was struck and the spring burst forth:

> One of the soldiers pierced his side with a spear, and at once blood and water came out. (He who saw this has testified so that you also may believe. His testimony is true, and he knows that he tells the truth.) (John 19:34-35)

In the resurrection the disciples find their own desire for God, and God's will bursts forth. The Spirit that impassioned Jesus wells up in their hearts.

Before we plunge into the celebration of the Passion and Resurrection, we do well to pass by the fig tree once more.

> In the morning as they passed by, they saw the fig tree withered away to its roots. Then Peter remembered and said to him, "Rabbi, look! The fig tree that you cursed has withered." Jesus answered them, "Have faith in God." (Mark 11:20-22)

Mark wants to confront us once more with this image of sterility and death. What Jesus pronounces useless is dead and death-dealing. Much of what passes as religion, as wisdom, as sound politics, is dead. Jesus has told us not to take it in any more. At the heart of repentance is the honesty to call dead things dead.

The church completes the irony by pointing to the other dead tree in the story, the dead tree of the cross. In contrast to the withered fig tree, this tree is superbly alive, gloriously fruitful. Our hymns extol it in lyrics of paradisal abundance, the one and only noble tree with which none can compare in foliage, blossom, and fruit.

Once this used to embarrass me. I thought it was an attempt to smother the harsh reality of the cross with the florid rhetoric of glory. But life, passion, bliss, desire is the fire Christ came to kindle on earth. It is our deadness and sterility the cross kills, not our life. What we risk by drawing near to the cross is not dying. We risk coming alive.

Crossing Over

T he expression "bearing one's cross" has become a feeble, pious commonplace, a trite metaphor for resigning oneself to some unavoidable burden or misfortune. My grandmother would refer to a neighbor with an alcoholic husband or a mentally retarded child with a doleful shake of her head: "That's the cross she has to bear!" We have retained Jesus' words but drastically altered their meaning. What a travesty it would be if we dared to attribute our threadbare sentiment about pious resignation to the Jesus revealed by St. Mark's gospel, whose words are like a violent flash of lightning revealing in a few seconds of terrible clarity the real meaning of discipleship, which will be finally disclosed and sealed by Jesus' crucifixion!

The image of taking up the cross was not some esoteric symbol for Jesus, but a horrible reality of daily life in an enemy-occupied country. No one could travel about Palestine for very long without coming across pitiful processions of condemned criminals, naked, bloody, dragging the crossbars to the places of execution. Crucifixion was a hideous torture reserved for slaves, terrorists, the dregs of humanity, and was part of the machinery of repression of the Roman administration. It was particularly horrifying and repulsive to Jews because the divine law of Moses pronounced a special curse damning these victims.

Why were the condemned forced to take up their crosses and drag them through the streets on the way to the killing fields? No doubt it intensified their degradation to be subjected to the abuse and loathing of the passersby, and it also gave the public an opportunity to disown the victims. As they pelted the victims with filth and jeers, the law-abiding populace could be strengthened in their own sense of rectitude. In this way, between the criminals about to be nailed to the crosses and the decent citizens going about their business a great gulf was fixed.

On the road to Caesarea Philippi Jesus told his disciples that if they wanted to know who he really was, they had to accept that he was the Son of man who was going to suffer. He intended to cross over the gulf, to leave once and for all the company of the upright and decent and to join those under sentence of death. Peter reacted as if Jesus had kicked him in the stomach, and Jesus came back at him with equal vehemence: "Get behind me, Satan!" If Peter tries to hold him back from this crossing over, he will become the very devil—Jesus' adversary, not his disciple. So they had better get this right. It was not for Jesus alone; anyone who wanted to follow him into true life had to cross over, too. Anyone who wanted to be identified with Jesus and find life with him had to join him in the procession of the condemned, the dying, and the rejected.

Six days after this bombshell Peter, James, and John had the experience we call the Transfiguration. Three days after Jesus actually had crossed over, crucified on Skull Hill with two criminals, God raised him from death, confirming once and for all that the business of crossing over, of taking up one's cross, is the real way into life.

This revelation was a bombshell then and it is a bombshell now, but it is not as though Jesus hasn't prepared us for it. He was constantly painting pictures of men and women who would not let go, who would not cross over but clung to their self-image of decency and self-sufficiency and security. The story of the Pharisee and the tax collector at prayer in the temple springs to mind. The Pharisee is secure in his sense of rectitude, full of gratitude to God for knowing what is right and being able to do it. He thanks God for being on the right side of the gulf that separates him from the miserable collaborator, the quisling tax collector weeping over his sins. The sting of Jesus' story is that the Pharisee is on the wrong side of the gulf. God is with the tax collector in his sorrow and impotence. If the Pharisee was to find God, he would have to cross over to the other side and find himself needy before God, dependent on his mercy.

God is with those who know that life is precarious and lived in immediate, moment-by-moment dependence on him. Many other stories tell of those who will not forgive another's debts, those who cannot cross over to the side of the needy, those who refuse to regard themselves as needy and thus turn on the unsuccessful and dependent with harshness and rejection.

Jesus is with us now, inviting us to cross over to him in the place of failure and poverty, to take up the cross. It is an invitation, a beckoning, not a threat. "Do you want life?" he asks us. "You will find it with me," he promises. But the rendezvous where he promises to meet us is where we are so reluctant to be—the place of failure. All I can say is that you don't need to step out of your own room to find the places of failure and need; they are within you. You are called to find them in the world, and to find Christ there, but it is useless to try to do that without finding them within yourself, and Christ there in them.

For some of you, it is time to cross over to the place within yourself of the failure to love. Self-hatred is everywhere, lodged in the hearts of those who come week by week to the altar. There are selves within us that we despise, that we cannot forgive, that appall us with their fantasies and disgust us with their weakness. Jesus has already crossed over to them, and it is time to have compassion on these ruined and sick parts of ourselves that he is embracing in the arms of his love. He is waiting for us to accept healing of our self-hatred. It is time to cross over and meet Jesus embracing the failed and ugly selves of the heart, and healing us.

For some of you, it is time to cross over to the place of neediness and vulnerability. Our culture idealizes self-sufficiency, individualism, secure arrangements that protect us from depending on one another. What we acclaim as virtues are exposed by the X-rays of the gospel to be signs of estrangement from the God who binds us into mutual dependence and love. The good news of Jesus permits us to be needy people who haven't got what it takes to love, haven't got what it takes to forgive, haven't got what it takes to make peace, haven't got what it takes to stay loyal, and so day after day must stretch out empty hands to God for what we need and can never deserve. The good news of Jesus permits us to be poor. For some of you it is time to wake up to your real needs and your real poverty, responding at long last to Jesus' constant urging: "Ask and it will be given you; seek and you will find; knock and it will be opened to you." If you don't ask, you are alienated from your own needs and still on the wrong side of the gulf that Jesus crossed over.

There is a third place of failure that lives in us all. No matter how successful our lives turn out to be, there is one place where we will all completely fail. We will all fail to stay alive. Of those on the brink of death we sometimes say, "It looks from her breathing as if she is really failing now." That is the place of failure we all come to, and the place to which Jesus crossed over when he took up his cross. An enormous proportion of human endeavor goes to numbing the pain of this prospect of utter failure with anesthetics like alcohol, drugs, overwork, and time-killing projects that give the appearance of a full life. But in fact full life is exclusively reserved for those who look deeply into the face of death and ask the question, "Do I amount to nothing?" The resurrection of Jesus and the meeting in the heart with the Jesus who is risen give the answer to men and women of faith. The resurrection says, "In death you fall into the arms of a God who loves you absolutely. So go and live, go and let go. No need either for pain-killers or self-projects. You are the desire of God's heart."

The difference this makes, the discovery that you are the desire of God's heart, is not like being born again. It *is* being born again. It is to rise from the dead *now*. It is time for us to cross over with Jesus into the place of death and discover it is the only place where we can truly come alive.

Do You Know What I Have Done to You?

Maundy Thursday, at the monastery

"**D**o you know what I have done to you?" We have no difficulty answering Jesus' question, since the gospel already puts the answer into our mouths: "You have given us an example. You performed this menial task for your disciples. We should be at one another's service in the same way." But in giving this ready-made answer we can keep ourselves out of the footwashing. We live in a shoe-wearing society, so to us footwashing is a quaint Bible-land custom, something slaves and servants did. We don't have servants; we have washing machines and showers and vacuum cleaners. The example has a folkloric remoteness.

But what if we are meant to plunge into the depths of the symbol and not merely draw a lesson from its exemplary surface? What if we were actually to experience being washed with our modern feelings and sensibilities? We can begin to grasp what this might mean by asking ourselves when was the last time we let anyone else wash our bodies. What memories might this question stir?

Some of you will be saying to yourselves, "Ah, the last time was when I was in love. We used to shower together. I remember the time when we lay for hours in that vast bathtub by candlelight, letting in more hot water now and then." And others will be thinking, "Oh, I was so sick and sore in hospital. What relief when the nurse came round to give me my bedbath. How strange it was not to be able to help her. How restorative it was, and how fresh I felt afterward." Others will have to ponder in their imaginations a time before memory, with themselves as little babies splashing their hands in the bathwater as their mothers patiently sponged them, or that first bath after being born. Being washed is almost the first thing that happened to us after we were born, as it will be the last thing after we have died.

"Do you know what I have done to you?" If we allowed ourselves to go to the root of our experience of being washed, then we might cry from the heart to Christ in answer to his question, "Yes, Lord, I know what you have done to me. In your death and resurrection you are my new mother giving me rebirth, new being. From you I emerge a new self, a new creation by water and the Spirit."

"Yes, Lord, I know what you have done to me. While I was yet helpless, at the right time, you died for me. When I was powerless to love, unable to heal myself, you became my healer and my nurse, cleansing away the sweat and grime of my folly and moral sickness, refreshing my fatigue and fever, invigorating my lassitude with love and forgiveness and the anointing of the Holy Spirit."

"Yes, Lord, I know what you have done to me. You have taken me to yourself in an embrace from which I shall never be thrust away. In the cross, having loved me who am in the world, you loved me to the end. Now it is I who am the beloved disciple and my place is always as close as it is possible to be—leaning upon your breast."

"Do you know what I have done to you?" Christ has given us an example in his footwashing but the example is the tip of the iceberg. Beneath is the vast bulk and depth of meaning of what Christ has done for us in that self-giving to the uttermost, what Christ has done to each of us as if we were the only man or woman in the world. The symbol and event that dominates this vastness of meaning is baptism.

Baptism is an event that is done to us. No one can baptize herself or himself. Baptism is done to us to convey what Christ did to us while we were yet helpless. Christ crucified and risen has given birth to us, to our new selves reconciled to the God of Love. Christ has washed and healed us of guilt. Christ has freely taken us to himself in an intimacy without shame, a new naked innocence of prayer and closeness, he in us and we in him, which regrounds our life in unconditional love.

The evangelist expects us to search out the baptismal symbolism by picking up the clue of Peter's misunderstanding and Jesus' reply.

> "Unless I wash you, you have no share with me." Simon Peter said to him, "Lord, not my feet only but also my hands and my head!" Jesus said to him, "One who has bathed does not need to wash, except for the feet, but is entirely clean. And you are clean, though not all of you." (John 13:8-10)

These cryptic words become intelligible when we realize that they are John's way of saying that baptism is our once-and-for-all washing. We are clean all over—unless, like Judas, we have turned against Christ in apostasy. Because of our baptism, we never need to start over again from nothing with Christ. We know what Christ has done to us—taken us once and for all into his union with his Father and our Father, his God and our God.

But is it not true that our need cries out to be met again and again? Is it not true that day by day and week by week we need a fresh experience of our rebirth as new selves, we need healing and cleansing from the grime and illness of today, we need a renewed embrace of intimacy to solve our fear and separateness? Of course it is. The washing of the feet is the symbol of that ever-repeated, ever-new reactivation of Christ's self-giving, the eucharist. John chooses not to describe the inauguration of the eucharist at the Last Supper, but instead to symbolize it in the footwashing: "He who has bathed does not need to wash except for his feet." Those who been baptized do not need to be baptized again; they have been born again and Christ is in them and they in Christ. But they do need to be served again by Christ the servant, and they do need to let love reenvelop them and heal them and reestablish them. They need the eucharist, which is love available not just once but again and again until the end.

"Do you know what I have done to you?" Tonight when you have fed on Christ in the bread and the cup, look down at him at your feet and hear him ask you, "Do you know what I have done to you?" Do not hide behind silence. Answer him. Tell him what you know. "Christ, I know what you have done to me today, what you do to me week by week. In this holy eating and drinking you reenter the bloodstream of my being, you unite yourself afresh with me. You nourish what is needy in me, you cleanse what is soiled, you embrace back to life my inmost self that halts and falters on its journey to fullness. You have given me yourself, and so, being found again inseparable from you, I find myself in God and with God, where I belong."

No More Tears

T wo things my family could have done with were psycho-
therapy and central heating, but we could afford neither.
The time-honored English substitute was long hot baths in
which you could keep warm while sorting out jangled feelings
and meditating on the deeper concerns of life. Bathtime meditation has not passed altogether out of my life and for a long
time I have been meditating on the label of the Johnson's
Baby Shampoo bottle standing next to the faucets.

The idea of a baby invites thoughts about being born again
and accepting the kingdom of God as a child, but there is also
the motto in the corner of the bottle: *No more tears!* Sometimes the meditation takes the form of a rebuke: Stop that stupid self-pity! Sometimes it is an assurance that something
painful is healed now. Then it points to the promise of the
kingdom of God when all the agonies of humankind will be
healed, and the blissful hand of God will, as the Book of Revelation puts it, "wipe every tear from their eyes. Death shall be
no more" (21:4).

A whole world of meaning opens up only when we press on
with this question of tears and ask, "Is it only on human faces
that there are tears of suffering and pain?" What of the eternal
face of God? Does God suffer? Does this promise of no more
tears apply only to us, or is it a promise that the pain of God

and the tears of God's own suffering will be overcome by bliss at the last? The suffering of God is one of the deepest mysteries of the Christian faith. Those who hear about it for the first time are often shocked, for this mystery doesn't lie on the surface of the scriptures, but deep down, and it takes some digging below the surface to reach the bedrock of this strange truth.

Let us take today's gospel and dig down beneath the surface. Luke shows Jesus determined to bring his prophetic ministry to a climax in the temple at Jerusalem. He knows that this showdown will result in his being killed. Now as Jesus pauses on his journey, his anguish over this inevitable rejection overflows in a passionate outburst:

> Jerusalem, Jerusalem, the city that kills the prophets and stones those who are sent to it! How often have I desired to gather your children together as a hen gathers her brood under her wings, and you were not willing! (Luke 13:34)

Now, on the surface it might seem as if Jesus were simply exclaiming that on several occasions during the past two years he has wanted to go to the capital city and bring everyone together in reconciliation under the blessing of the good news of forgiveness. But in fact this outburst of Jesus is more daring than that. If you ponder it deeply you will realize that Jesus is speaking for God, expressing the feelings of God, just as the prophets of old used to do. It is God who is like a hen tenderly yearning to gather her scattered chicks under the protection of her wings. It is God who for generations, for centuries, has sent envoy after envoy to reconcile and convert his people, only to meet repudiation and hostility.

Jesus adopts a special idiom used by Jewish wisdom teachers. In Old Testament books like Proverbs these teachers personified the Wisdom of God as a wonderfully attractive and brilliant woman who stands in public beseeching the passersby to forsake folly and lawlessness and to come into her home, where she will nourish and console and guide them. These teachers loved startling images. So Jesus now follows them and assumes the role of God's passionate, motherly tenderness and care which is so consistently refused by men and women wedded to their obstinate lovelessness and ignorance.

The words of Jesus testifying to the pain of God's heart don't go much farther than those of the prophets, but the preaching of the first Christians did. In the agony and crucifixion of Jesus God was not hurt merely by sympathy with the latest prophet to be martyred. God suffered *in* Christ. The audacious teaching of the early Christians that Jesus was the Incarnation of God's Word and Wisdom had the staggering consequence of making the crucifixion on Golgotha God's climactic suffering at the hands of his own creatures.

In the Passion of the Son, God shows that he keeps company with us, is one with us in all the suffering that is built into our fallen human existence. Jesus identifies himself with the guilty. He dies the most degrading death, the culmination of a ministry in which he kept company with the sick, the possessed, the despised and devalued. His suffering and dying and descent into hell is God living our life.

Now this is radical stuff. This is nothing like what the man in the street thinks about God. In fact, our theologians have constantly shied away from saying the two words outright: God suffers. It has been the mystics and the artists of the church who have had the daring. One of the classic places it has been said in our tradition and century is in a famous scene from Helen Waddell's novel *Peter Abelard*, about the great theologian of the middle ages who was punished and exiled for his affair with his pupil Heloise. Abelard is with his companion Thibault in the woods and they come upon a dead rabbit mangled by a snare.

> He looked down at the little draggled body, his mouth shaking. "Thibault," he said, "do you think there is a God at all? Whatever has come to me, I earned it. But what did this one do?"

Thibault nodded. "I know," he said. "Only—I think God is in it too."

Abelard looked up sharply. "In it? Do you mean that it makes Him suffer, the way it does us?" Again Thibault nodded. "Then why doesn't He stop it?"

"I don't know," said Thibault....But all the time God suffers. More than we do."

Abelard looked at him, perplexed...."Thibault, do you mean Calvary?"

Thibault shook his head. "That was only a piece of it—the piece that we saw—in time. Like that." He pointed to a fallen tree beside them, sawn through the middle. "That dark ring there, it goes up and down the whole length of the tree. But you only see it where it is cut across. That is what Christ's life was; the bit of God that we saw. And we think God is like that, because Christ was like that, kind and forgiving sins and healing people. We think God is like that for ever, because it happened once, with Christ. But not the pain. Not the agony at the last. We think that stopped."

Abelard looked at him, the blunt nose and the wide mouth, the honest troubled eyes. He could have knelt before him. "Then, Thibault," he said slowly, "you think that all this," he looked down at the little quiet body in his arms, "all the pain of the world, was Christ's cross?"

"God's cross," said Thibault. "And it goes on."[1]

Maybe this Lent could be a time for you to ponder this mystery. It could help you realize how revolutionary the doctrine of the Incarnation is. If Jesus is nothing more than the greatest prophet of God, then we can leave God out of suffering in heaven. But if the Crucified is God, then God is revealed as the one who is with us in suffering. The concept of God as a remote and dispassionate observer is smashed as an idol.

What effect might it have on your own life to ponder this mystery? First, you may find your understanding of sin changing. We think of sin as a kind of lawbreaking or failure God observes from afar, with disapproval. But this is very much farther from the truth than the description of sin as *"grieving the Holy Spirit"* (Eph. 4:30). Sin is what we do to block and frustrate God's action in our lives. Sin is thwarting and injuring the loving presence of God in our hearts. Sin pokes God in the eye, kicks him in the stomach. We wound God in our hearts and God in our neighbor through our faithless apathy.

Second, you may find your way of thinking of God's presence in the world undergoing a change. If God suffers, then God truly can be recognized by faith as present everywhere in a creation that groans in travail. We will stop praying to God to pay attention to this suffering or that tragedy. God doesn't need to pay attention to suffering because he is already present in and with the sufferers, and from that place of pain is moving us to contribute our caring and loving to his.

Third, contemplating the mystery of God's cross will change the way we come to terms with our own pain. If we have explored the mystery beforehand we may, when sickness, death, betrayal, or disappointment befall us, be better prepared to see that God is not far from us, but keeps us company and continues to hold us up with those hands that from the beginning of time have been pierced with unimaginable nails.

But such is the mystery that all the seasons of Lent left to us in this life will not be enough to sound its depths. Only by seeing Christ in the glory of the Father with his hands, feet, and side still pierced with wounds will we grasp the mystery—or be grasped by it.

Notes
1. Helen Waddell, *Peter Abelard* (New York: The Literary Guild, 1933), 289-290.

Resurrection

Paschal Joke

W e are told that as late as the eighteenth century, when it came to preaching on Easter Day, Lutheran pastors in Germany still felt bound by an ancient rule. Custom prescribed that the sermon should begin with a joke, known as the *risus paschalis*, "the paschal joke." We can imagine the solemn pastor fiddling nervously with his starched ruff, pulling his face into a rare smile, and starting off his sermon with, "Have you heard the one about...?" or, "A funny thing happened on my way to...."

They say that botanists have managed to grow plants from seeds found wrapped in the mummies of Pharaohs, and perhaps this obsolete custom entombed in church history also has life in it yet. Why a joke, we might ask? For those who have ears to hear, the joke tells us that what follows—the proclamation of the empty tomb and the resurrection of Jesus—is a joke God plays on us. In one way it is impossible to take the resurrection seriously. Really, it is laughable, isn't it? Or is it? Do we get God's joke or not? Let's see....

Death is no laughing matter and never has been. Nor is the dream of life beyond the grave anything but, to use a strangely telling pun, a grave business. Our forebears who invented agriculture found that their planting and reaping brought them to the brink of solemn mysteries. If the dry seed could be buried and then shoot up as a living plant and bear fruit, what about the corpses of men and women buried in the earth? So they buried trinkets, flowers, and weapons with their dead in some blind hope that the dying and rising of vegetation was a sign of life for us beyond the grave.

The symbol of resurrection found expression in myths of gods who died and came to life, in myths and rituals that encompassed seedtime and harvest, spring and fall, and in funerals that closed short human lives and wove around them dreams of paradise. By Jesus' day the lines were already drawn, much as we find them today, between those who condemned the symbol as illusory and deceptive and those who pinned their hopes on it. The Sadducees were conservatives who urged people to mistrust the prospect of resurrection as a fantasy conjured up to evade the finality of death, while the Pharisees insisted on resurrection as a remote prospect, taking place at the end of time, far beyond the here and now. Above all, resurrection was the precondition for the last judgment: God would have to raise the dead if all were to be present at the Great and Universal Trial.

Resurrection—a disputed question and an ambiguous symbol expressing human ambivalence about the finality of death. We human beings accept death and yet we cannot help projecting into some distant, mythic future the possibility of restoration to life, in the symbol of the rising of the body from the grave.

And on a particular Sunday morning, God did something absurd in the face of all this human solemnity about death. God took our symbol literally. In a strange work that flies in the face of our sense of propriety, with a scandalous literalness that offends our sense of the spiritual, God said, "Oh, is resurrection troubling you? Well, here goes. I'll start with Jesus. Now you see him, now you don't. One grave empty, the rest to follow."

The joke is that human beings like their symbols to stay symbolic. That is why a book comes out every year, and has been doing for a hundred years or so, and says that of course the story of the empty tomb is a "legend." The writers all adopt the same injured tone. The resurrection should stay symbolic. It should symbolize the enduring and uplifting effect of Jesus' teaching in the hearts of believers, or express pictorially the belief that Jesus is now spiritually exalted. All of these writers are exasperated by the embarrassing naiveté of the common run of preachers and faithful who keep on celebrating the emptiness of the tomb. It infuriates them that we don't get the message—that resurrection is so obviously appropriate as a metaphor that there was no reason at all for anything special to happen to Jesus' corpse.

But maybe those of us who believe in the empty tomb are not merely credulous. Maybe we are just captivated by the audacity of the divine humor. Who but the odd God of Jesus would think of such a ploy and make resurrection blow an empty hole in the middle of human history and human thought? Resurrection not as a myth about the end of time but a reality punched into the midst of time, right here where we are.

The crucifixion and burial are about human power over God. We took God's expression of God's very self, nailed it down, and buried it. We took the Son of God and nailed him down and buried him. And then just when we thought we had him contained and secure in the tomb, suddenly the stone is rolled back and…nothing. Gone! The whole business is in terribly bad taste, as if God were to play Houdini. God gets free. The grave is empty, and the shroud and headcloth are folded neatly, as the gospel asserts with shameless implausibility. The Lord of all creation seems to wink at us, behaving like a thoughtful houseguest who doesn't leave the bedclothes in a mess when she leaves.

Jesus is free to leave, and that means we lost. We couldn't pin him down or shut him up even by dragging him into our death. But this is a very strange game. By losing, we win. The outcome is a sign that God is free to punch a hole in the fabric of our entire reality and that God intends us all to pass through this hole into his arms. This hole is the siphon through which all of us and all that we are will be drawn into the life and being of God. "I am ascending to my Father and your Father, to my God and your God."

By losing, we win. The joke of the resurrection is on us. God takes our resurrection symbol literally, just here, just once, for Jesus. But you either get a joke or you don't. If you get the joke, and start to laugh, then the "Of-course-the-tomb-wasn't-actually-empty" line seems prudish and humorless in its distaste for the solid food of God's brash, hearty, gross, and even comic act.

I remember a reproduction of an engraving I once saw in the style of Dürer that showed the Risen Lord at the moment when Mary Magdalene thought he was the gardener. It is impossible not to smile at this artwork because Jesus is sporting a straw sun hat with a huge, floppy brim. Of course Mary thinks he is the gardener: he's got gardener's clothes on!

These strange embellishments of the core testimony to the empty tomb—stories of passing through doors, eating fish, popping up on the road to Emmaus, playing hide-and-seek with Mary in a gardener's disguise in the morning half-light—are all strange and comical stories. They are the stories of people who feel a lighthearted freedom to make the joke they have heard even funnier in the retelling.

It is my custom on Easter Day to recite to myself some strange words of Samuel Taylor Coleridge:

If a man should pass through Paradise in a dream,
and have a flower presented to him as a pledge
that his soul had really been there,
and if he found that flower in his hand
when he awoke—Ay, and what then?

It seems to me that this is what the empty tomb is like for us. Paradise, the paradise of God, of eternity, of peace, is a dream. But one morning a group of women and men woke up in a garden and found in their hand the flower from Paradise, the sign that we dream what is there, what is waiting for us, what is absolutely real. The empty tomb, the folded cloths, these are the flower we wake to find in our hand each Easter morning. We are very funny people, we Christians, who have this dream as our only defense against death and despair. We find that this dream is all we need to walk on with the smile of those who hope.

Once again, in just three days, we have experienced the transformation of the drama of our lives. It began with the melodrama of we poor innocents, victims with Jesus of misunderstanding and hostility. Then it changed to tragedy: we discovered that the worst enemy is within and we ourselves are the betrayers and the killers of love. We are the crucifiers. And now it has been changed by God to comedy in the resurrection. We have been shown the comic *dénouement* of harmony and happiness. Our lives are not melodramas or tragedies, but scenes in a divine comedy which, by a thousand detours and setbacks, will bring us all round together in the end into the endless dance of the communion of saints.

God's Strange Work

T here is real irony in the fact that the gospel appointed for St. Mark's day is from that very part of the book which he certainly did not write. The closing paragraph of St. Mark's gospel we are used to is one of several attempts by well-meaning scribes to round the gospel off. It is, to be honest, a rather clumsy pastiche, with its odd and superstitious-sounding references to immunity from snake-venom and poisons.

So how did the gospel originally end? To our alarm we discover that the book originally ended with these words: "So they went out and fled from the tomb, for terror and amazement had seized them; and they said nothing to anyone, for they were afraid" (Mark 16:8). In the Greek the ending sounds even more abrupt: *ephobounto gar,* "they were terrified, you see."

Pitiable attempts have been made to suggest that Mark's original happy ending got lost, like when a detective story you've taken on vacation gets so battered around that to your horror you discover the last two pages have come loose and blown away. Or there is the picture, worthy of an old Hollywood costume Bible epic, of Mark furiously scribbling away to finish the gospel and just as he gets to the last page there is a knock on the door and the Roman soldiers take him off to the Colosseum while a maid quickly grabs the manuscript and hides it in the folds of her ample bosom.

The hard truth is that Mark deliberately ended the gospel on an agonizing note of suspense, fear—and we must not hesitate to say it out loud—disobedience. The young man in a white robe tells the women not to be amazed. But they are amazed, and more than amazed, they are scared witless. They give way to *tromos* and *ekstasis*; a colloquial translation would be "They completely lost it." The angel tells them to "Go, tell his disciples and Peter that he is going ahead of you to Galilee; there you will see him, just as he told you" (Mark 16:7). But they do not do this because they are too frightened. The Greek says, "They told nothing to no one."

Is it any wonder that the later gospel writers, disturbed by this abrupt and shocking ending, preferred other versions of what happened on the first day of the week in which the women did tell the other disciples? Is it any wonder that scribes concocted additional paragraphs from traditions of other Easter appearances and added them to the manuscripts of Mark's gospel to soften the impact?

We should not be surprised at all that Mark ended his book, whose very form was his invention, on the heart-searching note of human fear and disobedience in the face of God's acting through Jesus. The theme is woven into every page. Mark as narrator is always commenting on the action with asides such as, "He charged them to tell no one; but the more he charged them, the more zealously they proclaimed it." "They did not understand the saying and were afraid to ask him." The Christ of Mark's gospel is always in an agony of frustration at the inability of the disciples to get the picture. "O faithless generation, how long am I to be with you?" "Get behind me, Satan! for you are not on the side of God, but of men." Mark has such an intense awareness of human ignorance and resistance even in the very face of God's own beloved Son, the Servant who came to give his life as a ransom for many, that he chose to end the good news on a discordant note, without a resolution. That way we readers are left to probe our hearts and see whether we are too paralyzed and afraid to be empowered and jubilant at the news of the resurrection.

Of course the other evangelists have their own integrity in the way they conclude their gospels with the stories of the appearances of Christ, but Mark still has a role to play in the dialectic of our struggle with the mystery of resurrection. Let us call him the perennial critic of cheap triumphalism. God raised Jesus from the dead, and took a risk in doing so, because right from the beginning this resurrection could be taken over by the human lust for mythic reassurance in the face of winter and death. The dying and rising God is a theme as old as the hills—or as old as the fields, as old as agriculture. Of course new life follows on death in an endless cycle. This proclamation of the resurrection of Jesus would say that everything is going to be all right, that new life springs out of the old, heaven will follow automatically after our earthly phase, good will come out of bad, light from dark, spring from winter.

"To hell with all that" is Mark's response. In the resurrection of Jesus we are not dealing with mythic inevitability and comfort, but a strange and shocking act of God that defies human expectations and stuns us by its momentous and undreamed of implications. The theologians and reformers of the church used to apply to the event of Christ's death and resurrection a phrase taken from Isaiah that speaks of the *opus alienam* of God, "God's strange work." The phrase is the quintessence of the Markan vision. His gospel ends on the note not of human reassurance and solace, but of stunned amazement. God has raised Jesus from death. The resurrection of the dead has occurred and this new reality has exploded within our present world and time instead of bringing it all to an end.

So Mark dares not narrate the stories of the appearances for fear we would latch on to them as an excuse for turning our backs on the cross. The terror of the women is intended to evoke our fear in the face of a happening for which God alone could be responsible, an event that specifically designates the crucified Servant as the chosen of God. Now there is no way out of Jesus' proclamation of suffering servanthood as the very life of God, and the very life we are to live. God has set his seal on this interpretation of reality divine and human, on this interpretation alone, by unwinding the bandages from the bloody corpse of the victim of the cross and transfiguring it into the glorified state of the life to come. It is terrifying before it is consoling. The great stone rolls away from the entrance to the grave, but it blocks the path of our cheap and easy substitutes for suffering love, which we want to call divine.

A great British theologian, Donald McKinnon, who used to be a server at our Society's church in Oxford and was a sharp critic of our mistakes, recalled in a great essay on the atonement and tragedy "the extent to which in popular apologetic understanding of the resurrection has been deformed through its representation as in effect a descent from the cross given greater dramatic effect by a thirty-six hour postponement."[1] This sentence lodged in my mind like a burr twenty years ago. Think about it. It always sends me back to Mark's gospel, the enemy of cheap grace, liturgical myth-making, cultic reassurance. Christ did not descend from the cross. Christ has still not descended from the cross.

Did you know that early tradition handed on a peculiar memory of Mark's physical build? The early church historians say he had the nickname "stumpy-fingered." That figures, doesn't it? Mark's gospel was the creation not of an aesthete, but of a man with a powerful and even intricate imagination who was consumed by a passion for hard-hitting truth.

So today on his feast day we offer our thanksgiving with angels and archangels and with all the company of heaven, and unite our hearts with Mark, who is alive in Christ and prays for us. We can picture him gripping a pen with stumpy fingers and tracing the words *ephobounto gar*, "they were terrified, you see," on the papyrus. And then stopping. Letting the ink dry and saying, "That's where I'm ending!"

There was no such thing as a gospel a few months before but now there is and that is how it ended. Now that scholarship has taught us to put brackets round the later, softer, more muddled ending, those who have ears to hear will understand why. They will be galvanized again by the shocking force of God's strange work in raising the Crucified from the dead, and moved to compunction over their disobedience and fear.

Notes

1. Donald McKinnon, *Borderlands of Theology*, ed. G. W. Roberts and D. E. Smucker (London: Lutterworth Press, 1968), 100.

Adam

The eucharist of the resurrection celebrating the life of Adam Fifer, SSJE, at the monastery, October 26, 1994

W here exactly were you when you heard of the assassination of Adam's hero, John F. Kennedy? Everyone in America above a certain age can say, and even I can remember that I was at boarding school in England fixing a Chinese meal on the gas ring outside my study. Perhaps in years to come we will all remember just what we were doing when we heard that Adam's long-awaited death had finally come. I was in a moonlit plaza in old San Juan, and not long after that Brother Brian and I were talking about Adam as we wandered at dusk in the gardens of an old hacienda in the Uroyan Mountains. We stopped at one point to look at orchid blossoms that had fallen from the trees onto the red, red earth, and as I lay awake that night that simple sight spoke to me about the wonderful human being whose loss we are mourning, whom we are handing over to God.

Now Adam was a rare bloom, don't you think? A very distinctive, even exotic character. Instinctively Carl has massed a bright, even tropical display of flowers. I was going to suggest putting some of Adam's pink flamingos among the flowers but he had beaten me to it; they were there already. Adam was comfortable with his own originality and no superior would have wanted to tame the luxuriant decor of his cell or alter his inimitable style of preaching, with its brilliant recreations of scenes from his childhood, such as tent revival services, and his great exposition of the allegorical meaning of *The Wizard of Oz.* His devotion to his mother, his hero worship of President Kennedy, his preference for all things Benedictine, his deftness with the sewing machine and the computer, his long, chatty letters and conversations....

Yet there was another side to this airy, colorful character. He chose a monastic name, Adam, the first name of all, and I thought of this name as I looked down at the red earth. The Hebrew name Adam is a pun; in all the ancient languages of the Near East the sound *adamah* refers to the red, red earth. For some deep reason Michael Fifer chose the name that suggests the common earth, the blood red clay that is our common source. He wanted a name suggesting the whole race, our common origin in the shaping force of God's hand, our common vulnerability, our shared fallenness, our shared need for redemption.

Deliberately or not, he could hardly have adopted the name Adam without evoking our ancient mythic memory of fallenness, our expulsion from the garden of innocence into a wild world of struggle where every birth costs pain. He too bore the marks of our fallenness; twice he left the monastic community where he was working out his salvation. Then he learned that in a past phase of his life the HIV virus had entered his body and he was called to walk with so many millions of others this new and terrible stretch of the road of human suffering.

In the last week of his life Adam insisted that he would not wear clothes. It didn't make nursing him any easier, but like Francis of Assisi he needed nakedness in the end. In fact he had been willing all along to be naked in his humanness and his faith. Adam was a deft tailor but he didn't make himself any disguise or cover up who he was or what he was suffering. He simply clothed himself in faith with Christ, whom the scriptures call the Second Adam. He didn't find any new-fangled way to cope; he wore that old-time gospel of the cross of Christ, which he had responded to as a boy, and this old-time way, the monastic life. When we received Adam back into the community and he put his monastic habit back on, it was really only an outer sign of that inner clothing we all saw on him with the eyes of our faith.

Do you need me to remind you how powerfully he witnessed to the reality of God's grace and mercy as he moved steadily along his path? Adam lived this reliance on God artlessly, truthfully, humorously, winningly, patiently. Apparently busy with the administrative work he did so well, he was actually quite an apostle. His faith sustained his life longer than anyone had dared expect, right until he could take part in the liturgy of Tom's consecration as bishop, a great moment of fulfillment for all of us. Then he promptly pulled up the pegs of his tent and stopped taking medicine and food. He was ready to go home.

Death is surrounded by many clichés. It is so undoing, so disorienting, that we comfort each other with stereotypical words of consolation. In Adam's case the desire to go home to be with Jesus was simply and straightforwardly that. It burst the bounds of cliché and was a direct expression of the heart's desire.

The story of human redemption starts with God calling out to Adam in his hiding place in the garden. It reaches its climax in the mystery of the resurrection of Christ from the dead, portrayed so gloriously in the Easter icon that shows him trampling on the gates of death and pulling Adam and Eve out of their imprisonment and into the light of God. This is what we are here to celebrate today. This is the resurrection in which Adam is sharing. Adam drew people; he drew their love out of them. He isn't going to stop now. He is drawing us now into the reality of the risen life, asking us to accept it, live by it, and make hope the core of our life.

The day before yesterday Brian and I were immersed in a hot spring at Coamo that the Spanish conqueror Ponce de Leon believed was the Fountain of Eternal Youth. It was very nice, but one thing was perfectly clear to us—it wasn't going to work. These bodies of ours are bound for death. Our hope is not in arresting decay, but in a new act of creation in Christ: a new spiritual body that is already ours through our baptism into his body and our feeding on his body and blood in the eucharist. These bodies of flesh are clay, meant for the earth, until the great day when everyone has their new and eternal body of glory.

And so we ready ourselves to lay Adam's slight remains back into the earth, the earth we all come from, the earth his name refers to. I think he would be pleased if we did it with some majestic words still sounding in our ears from an early Christian poet called Prudentius. They were set to music by Herbert Howells to commemorate President Kennedy, Adam's hero.

Take him, earth, for cherishing,
To thy tender breast receive him.
Body of a man I bring thee,
Noble even in its ruin.

Once was this a spirit's dwelling,
By the breath of God created.
High the heart that here was beating,
Christ the prince of all its living.

Guard him well, the dead I give thee,
Not unmindful of His creature
Shall He ask it: He who made it
Symbol of His mystery.

Come the hour God hath appointed
To fulfill the hope of men,
Then must thou, in very fashion,
What I give return again.

Not though ancient times decaying
Wear away these bones to sand,

Ashes that a man might measure
In the hollow of his hand.

Not through wandering winds and idle,
Drifting through the empty sky,
Scatter dust was nerve and sinew,
Is it given man to die.

Once again the shining road
Leads to ample Paradise;
Open are the woods again
That the Serpent lost for men.

Take, O take him, mighty Leader,
Take again thy servant's soul,
To the house from which he wandered
Exiled, erring, long ago.

But for us, heap earth about him,
Earth with leaves and violets strewn,
Grave his name, and pour the fragrant
Balm upon the icy stone.

By the breath of God created
Christ the prince of all its living
Take, O take him,
Take him, earth, for cherishing.[1]

Notes
1. From Helen Waddell, *Mediaeval Latin Lyrics* (London/New York: Constable/Barnes and Noble, 1929/1966), 45.

We Were With Him on the Mountain

Requiem eucharist for James Madden, SSJE,
at the monastery, August 7, 1989

With God's help today we shall be able to make room in our hearts for all the pain that is trying to well up. This awful pain at James's death is a good friend and has something important to tell us. It wants to let us know that our lives are meshed together, not solitary, separate, or lonely. God has bound us together and is weaving our lives intricately together in the fabric of Christ, so that the death of this brother, this friend, this son, wrenches and stresses every fiber of our being. With God's help we shall not fight the pain or try to relax the stress and wrenching that is cutting into our very hearts.

The pain is confirming the good news that we are a communion of saints, a web of lives, a "tunic without seam, woven from the top to the bottom" by the Triune God of love. The shuttle has flown, the weaver's beam has slammed down, and the man we loved has been finally woven into the woof of the great communion. There is so much pain in this weaving. Who could bear it unless God had revealed on the cross that his pain is what is holding the world-loom together until the work is all finished and the "heavens can be rolled up like a garment," because they will be nothing compared to the glory of what God is making out of us all in his Son? So talking of the communion of saints now, and talking of James will help us know it for the truth it is.

God chose his pattern for James out of the book of life early on. He was born on St. James's Day in 1950 and given that saint's name—a saint who left everything for companionship with Jesus among the disciples. The disciple who was chosen for intimacy with Jesus that culminated on the Mount of Transfiguration, who was taken suddenly in the prime of life from his brothers and friends in a martyr's death. And now it is 1989 and James has died in his very prime between St. James's Day and the Feast of the Transfiguration.

After he died, I thought of the scripture passage from the second letter of Peter in which the surviving witness writes of that experience of glory:

> For he received honor and glory from God the Father when that voice was conveyed to him by the Majestic Glory, "This is my Son, my Beloved, with whom I am well pleased." We ourselves heard this voice come from heaven, while we were with him on the holy mountain. (2 Peter 1:17-18)

These words of a survivor became mine, "We were with him on the holy mountain." We who survive James want to tell you that we have seen transfiguration with him. We have seen the glory of God in his company, and the beauty of God in his.

James was destined to carry about in his body a lot of dying, a virulent form of cancer, and with a mysterious, balancing providence God endowed him with great beauty of face, of body, and of voice. He was so good to look at! Did you know that retreatants here at the monastery have actually had to be sent home because they couldn't stop looking at him? And he was so good to hear. That voice—singing, reading, talking over the phone, serious or merry, very lovely it was. He was good to touch in a brother's embrace in moments sad and happy, and in the liturgical actions he loved and did with such grace. We saw beauty in his calligraphy, his painting, the way he adorned the chapel for the feast. And God was in all that, attracting us through it all.

Jesus chose for his special companions two brothers, James and John, whom he nicknamed "sons of thunder." Well, we lived with one! He brought to life a strong flow of energy and the sparks could fly. Startled postulants would hear doors crash shut and then have to pick their way through fragments of pottery left from a mug hurled down the stairs. He was not one to suffer fools gladly; the fact is, he didn't suffer them at all. I have seen him crawl on his hands and knees out of church to avoid hearing any more of a sermon he couldn't tolerate, and as mysteriously reappear in time for communion.

His emotions ran in obscure Irish patterns difficult to construe, a source of passion that made him leave everything behind when he was very young to join a venerable community that many thought to be dying. This passion and energy carried him on to priesthood and made him a man continually growing. Some monks make great mothers and he was the best mother of souls—hours and hours of going the second mile with retreatants, directees, visitors, and the novices he loved. Hours in the night working through the piles of books with which he loved to surround himself. What energy he brought to the liturgy and how deceptive it all was, as if such caring came naturally! It was really grace and power in the strength of Christ whom he loved.

We saw the glory of God in suffering transfigured. Like Jesus on the mountain, he had to face the exodus he was to accomplish, knowing he would never reach old age. He lived the vocation of precarious life, uncertainty, pain, drastic procedures, surgeries, examinations. Over and over again we asked ourselves, "How does he do it?" but we never needed to answer because we knew.

The corner of his cell where he prayed was his home. Every month or so he would rearrange it from his array of lamps, icons, beads, books, cards, flowers, rugs, and cushions, but what never changed was the unflagging, unsentimental, struggling, heartfelt, contemplative gaze and conversation. Each of us in his own cell converged on the same place of divine love. We were with him on the holy mountain and we knew, although it never ceased to amaze us, where he derived the grace to transfigure his mortality so fully, with such humor and courage.

We were with him on the holy mountain, and he was with all of you in so many ways, his family and friends. What do we do now? On two occasions Jesus asked James and John and the other disciples to gather up the fragments that remained after he had fed multitudes in the wilderness. A strange request. What were they to do with all those bits and pieces left behind? I think Jesus was letting them learn something about a Creator who saves everything and loses nothing.

Already we are beginning to gather our memories of James, common memories and unique memories. Stories of childhood, of friendship, of his eccentricities and struggles, of his gifts and prejudices, of moments grave and gay, of his black humor and sweet wisdom. But they are only fragments, bits and pieces, and that is what is so agonizing. As we realize how fragmentary is our grasp of him, and mourn the loss of the inimitable man himself, we must look to God who has gathered him up, with nothing missing.

In Christ is his whole and real self risen up. In Christ the fruits of his life abide, everything he created and made possible and gave of himself, every way he fed others—all that is gathered up safely in Christ. Let our remembering, partial as it is, carry us in faith to Christ, whose gathering up of James is complete and entire. If we let this happen, the light of the future glory will shine through our memories and transfigure nostalgia into hope and absence into longing for reunion in the glorious body of Christ.

So we talk of the communion of saints today and sing of the resurrection, but we also welcome the pain and make room for it. If we open ourselves to the pain of this death, James can still do something very precious for us and help us get ready for our own dying. In recent weeks he let us know that he was readying himself for death, and as we take in the final surrender of his life, which we, his brothers and his family, witnessed, we can experience transfiguration here, too. The pain of letting go of him can help us prepare for the pain of letting go of ourselves, too, the losing of all footholds within ourselves in order to be possessed by God and woven finally into the communion of saints.

In the hospital waiting room a prayer from *The Divine Milieu* of Teilhard de Chardin kept rippling deep down in me:

> When the ill that is to diminish me or carry me off strikes from without or is born within me...above all at that last moment when I feel I am losing hold of myself and am absolutely passive within the hands of the great unknown forces that have formed me; in all those dark moments, O God, grant that I may understand that it is You (provided only my faith is strong enough) who are painfully parting the fibers of my being in order to penetrate to the very marrow of my substance and bear me away within Yourself....It is not enough that I should die while making my communion. Teach me to make my communion in dying.[1]

We have here at the eucharist our act of communion with the Lord and in him, with James. Thank God we have more than words.

Enough. Let us take the bread of life and the cup of salvation together and reembrace that Life which is James's now to the full, and is ours as we continue on the journey that has been so wonderfully graced by his companionship.

Notes

1. Teilhard de Chardin, *The Divine Milieu* (New York: Harper & Brothers, 1960), 62.

Soundings

Faith

This is the first in a series of three sermons on faith, hope, and love, those three gifts known to us so well from the thirteenth chapter of Paul's first letter to the church in Corinth. In fact, Paul linked them even earlier; these gifts are found together in the earliest text in the New Testament, Paul's first letter to the Thessalonians, written just about seventeen years after the resurrection, when the expectation of the imminent end of all things was very strong:

> But since we belong to the day, let us be sober, and put on the breastplate of faith and love, and for a helmet the hope of salvation. (1 Thess. 5:8)

Faith, hope, and love, Paul says, are the gifts to seek in the time of expectant interim, when the guarantees of stability and permanence are gone and all is in question.

Faith has not always meant the same thing. Consider how different the experience of faith was for our forebears in medieval Catholic Europe. There the opposite of faith was heresy. Faith was the given, revealed, and authorized version of reality. Faith was creed. Not to have faith was to be a threatening anomaly in society. Faith was what everyone must demonstrate in order to maintain an overarching sacred canopy of meaning. To question, to pose an alternative construction of reality, was madness, rebellion, a saboteur punching a hole below the water-line in the church's hull. There was a logic behind inquisition and crusade.

Consider how different again was the experience of our nineteenth-century forebears as the sacred canopy of meaning, the canonized Christian world-view, suffered a massive crisis of plausibility under the impact of science and modernity. Then the opposite of faith was doubt. To doubt was to feel implicated in the ebbing of general consent to the creeds. Individuals were plagued with doubt about doctrines like predestination to eternal condemnation in hell, about traditional Christology, about the authority of the scriptures. They were less convinced about certain elements of traditional Christianity, and the loss of part of the faith seemed to make them colluders in the general loss of religious conviction throughout early Victorian society. This is the moment captured in the 1851 poem "Dover Beach," by Matthew Arnold:

> The Sea of Faith
> Was once, too, at the full, and round earth's shore
> Lay like the folds of a bright girdle furled.
> But now I only hear
> Its melancholy, long, withdrawing roar,
> Retreating, to the breath
> Of the night-wind, down the vast edges drear
> And naked shingles of the world.
> Ah, love, let us be true
> To one another! for the world, which seems
> To lie before us like a land of dreams,
> So various, so beautiful, so new,
> Hath really neither joy, nor love, nor light,
> Nor certitude, nor peace, nor help for pain;
> And we are here as on a darkling plain
> Swept with confused alarms of struggle and flight,
> Where ignorant armies clash by night.

The poem foretells our condition, when we put so huge a weight of expectancy on what personal relationships can give—"Ah, love, let us be true to one another"—precisely because there is no longer a sacred canopy of meaning. That canopy has been torn up into rival constructions of reality, clashing value systems, "isms," and points of view, ignorant armies clashing by night. The poem already contains the seeds of the post-modern condition, which utterly lacks "certitude." Our version of doubt is not merely that the sea of faith has withdrawn. It is that we have come to realize with horror that there seems to be no longer any privileged standpoint for the assertion of truth at all. All standpoints seem merely relative, and every construction of reality, including the religious one of faith, is exposed as a virtuoso exercise of the human capacity for inventing webs of meaning.

In ancient times you did not choose to be religious; you simply were. In modern times people had to start choosing to be religious. In post-modern times we *know* that we are choosing. So our condition has been described by Peter Berger as "the vertigo of relativity"; the sickening disorientation that comes with the recognition that in adhering to one religious faith we are choosing from many, all of them equally open to criticism as culturally biased human projections.

If for our ancestors the opposite of faith was heresy, and for our great-grandparents the opposite of faith was doubt, for us the opposite of faith is certitude. Faith is now the exercise of a choice to interpret reality in terms of a loving God, in full, unblinking recognition of the fact that every particle of evidence that we call forth as signs of divine presence and activity can be and is everywhere interpreted in other terms. Faith is now seen to be creative, voluntary, not given and imposed. It is a choosing with others to see a certain way, to interpret from a certain perspective, to use a certain constellation of images and references to make meaning, while realizing all along that to claim a privileged access to truth by means of this faith-construction will be howled down from a dozen corners as groundless and arrogant.

To have religious faith is very strange these days because of its "man-bites-dog" aspect. For almost two centuries intellectuals have asserted that religious faith is a human construction and now we have to admit they are right. But now we turn round and say, "Yes, we project ultimate meanings onto the universe because the universe is ultimately meaningful. Creation intends and contains these meanings, so they spring up into our consciousness because we are grounded in them."

Here is the strangeness of it. We know we are choosing to construct reality a certain way, and yet we are bound by the imperious logic of belief in God to say that our constructs actually trace the lines of the way reality is constructed and are not just fanciful meanderings that happen to give us solace.

For us Christians it is tremendously healthy to realize that the opposite of faith is not doubt, but certitude. We don't have certitude and we do have doubt—lots of it. And doubt is not sick, not treacherous. As our founder, Father Benson, said, "The truest faith springs from really honest doubt." Doubt, doubt that returns often and is powerful, keeps us honest. A wise man once said, "I am grateful to my atheist friends, they keep me from cheating." Doubt is my inner atheist friend who reminds me that religious faith is not the obvious interpretation of reality. Doubt insists that I humbly remember that there are many other ways of accounting for our experience in the world. Doubt is an unsentimental teacher who flings the window open so that I feel the cold draft and hear the terrible screams from a world so fraught with suffering that it cannot see the hand of a compassionate creator. Doubt pulls our fingers from our ears to make us listen to snatches of songs and myths from faiths that undermine our insularity and denial.

When we realize that the opposite of faith is not heresy, not doubt, but certitude, we can read our own scriptures again with an original clarity. For the lynch-pin of our faith is what Paul called "the word of the cross," a phrase that hit its first hearers in the solar plexus. For them it meant what we might convey by saying, "The message about the electric chair, the message of the gallows." We interpret the reality of the universe by tracing the lines of meaning from the horrible execution of Jesus, whom we name the Son of God. This message, this construction of reality, is radically unsuited to be the orthodoxy of a society. It is intrinsically scandalous, too absurd to be accepted by most, let alone all. It requires a consent, a willingness, a profound yes. There is nothing about it that can coerce consent. It is a word so protective of our freedom that it is almost silent.

Let me give the last word to Paul Evdokimov, a lay Orthodox theologian, from his book *The Struggle with God*. He is speaking of the way God makes room for the free yes of faith.

Every compelling proof violates the human conscience and changes faith into simple knowledge. That is why [on the cross] God limits his almighty power, encloses himself in the silence of his suffering love, withdraws all signs, suspends every miracle, casts a shadow over the brightness of his face.

It is to this kenotic attitude of God that faith essentially responds. It keeps and will always keep an element of darkness, a crucifying obscurity, a sufficient margin to protect its freedom, in order to say *no* at any moment and to build on this refusal. It is because a man can say *no* that his *yes* can attain a full resonance; his fiat is then not only in accord with, but on the same dizzy level of free creation as the fiat of God.[1]

Notes

1. Paul Evdokimov, *The Struggle with God* (Glen Rock, N. J.: Paulist Press, 1966), 34.

Hope

I was sitting by the lake luxuriating in the leisure of my sab-
batical, smoking a cigar and studying Freud when I came
across a quotation from a letter he wrote to Marie Bonaparte.
"The moment a man questions the meaning and value of life,"
he said, "he is sick, since objectively neither has any existence." I looked up from the book and noticed there was absolute silence around me—and then the ducks on the lake broke
into a hysterical quacking as if to mock. "To us, he is no more
a person/Now but a whole climate of opinion," wrote W. H.
Auden about Freud. Perhaps these gray words of Freud are
one of the clues to the crisis in which we find ourselves as the
millennium draws to a close.

Freud, the great authority of western culture, asserts that
value and meaning are essentially unreal. To resign oneself to
their unreality, their lack of objective existence, is to be well.
To go on a quest for meaning and value is to fall sick. By now
we have a perspective from which we can see that that crisis of
meaninglessness is what our century's theater of the absurd
has been signalling all along in its decadent, joky way. The
plays of Beckett, Pinter, and Ionesco, as Vaclav Havel has said,
"throw us into the question of meaning by manifesting its absence. Absurd theater does not offer us consolation or hope. It
merely reminds us how we are living; without hope."

The experience of the absence of meaning and hopelessness are one and the same. Hope is about the creation of meaning, its fresh onset and its coming. So we must distinguish hope from two other phenomena.

First, hope has nothing in common with prediction, projection, and prognostication. It has no connection with futurology. Prediction claims that the future is so determined by the past that we can work out how it will grow out of the past. But we ought to know by now how limited is the range of interesting things that can be strictly predicted. Think, for example, of economics and how conflicting are the predictions emerging from rival practitioners—and how upsetting the actual turn of events. Hope has more to do with the unpredictability of the historical process. It is something that revives in us when fresh evidence of the unexpected comes in. Where were the predictions that Mandela and de Klerk would share the Nobel Peace prize?

Second, hope has nothing in common with optimism, a cheap, over-the-counter drug for maintaining denial. Hope is not only compatible with, but actually requires, a courageous facing of death and vulnerability. Hope is not having excuses for optimism; it is a strenuous expectation of creative newness and meaning in our lives.

The three virtues of faith, hope, and love used to be called "the theological virtues." This scholastic title sounds rather wooden, but it has its validity. All three virtues are intrinsically connected with belief in God. Let's see what this means with regard to hope. Hope is about the expectation of creative newness in our lives. It is faith in the meaningfulness of our personal and common future. Hope gives meaning to the present by conveying meaning about our future. But the simple fact is that the future does not exist; because it has not happened yet, it has no existence. Now, how can we have faith in something that does not exist?

The answer the gospel gives is this. We proclaim that God is the Being of all being, the Life of all life, the Source and Fulfillment of all. By God we mean the One who transcends space and time, or as we say, space-time. Our future is real in the One who is not confined within space and time but is infinite. Scripture spells this out in the liturgical proclamation that the God who accompanies us in time, nevertheless encompasses all time: "'I am the Alpha and the Omega,' says the Lord God, who is and who was and who is to come, the Almighty" (Rev. 1:8).

The gospel proclaims that God has created within time a means for the future that is real in him to seep into the present in order to change it in hope. The means is the death, burial, and resurrection of the beloved Son, Jesus. The empty tomb is a siphon that sucks the creative newness of God's future into our present so that our present can be changed by it—in Paul's pregnant words, "by hope we were saved" (Rom. 8:24). Hope is the irradiation of our present with the light of a future that is with and in God.

The secret of Christian identity is that faith in Christ and his future, faith in the reality of our future in him, is immeasurably stronger than the determinations of the past. From time immemorial human beings have interpreted their lives as determined by fate and doom and karma. They have "reified," as the philosophers say, made into external forces, their feelings of being determined and nailed down and controlled. Human beings have found comfort in supposing themselves powerless victims of the capricious turns of fortune's wheel, or controlled by astral forces in the sky.

Suddenly the resurrection of Jesus flooded his disciples with an irrepressible skepticism about every variety of this deterministic fantasy. How can there be any celestial principalities and powers jerking us around if simply by faith we can be united with God, whom nothing can control and defeat? How can we be doomed to extinction if here and now, simply by faith, we can be grafted into the life of God, with a graft that bodily death, far from snapping off, makes permanent and eternal? The resurrection made the disciples into blasphemers against religious determinism, the piety of fatalism. Remember, the early Christians were described by Greek and Roman religionists as "atheists" because their message was seen as essentially sacrilegious, dethroning the gods of control.

Hope, then, is the very core of Christian self-identity. I am not who the past dictates that I am. I am not wholly determined by my genes, not defined by my experiences in womb and family, nor identified with the complex of psychic and social influences that have gone into my making. I am not what others have decided I shall be. All these selves are not, to use that strange English expression, the "be all and end all" of myself. There is only one "be all," God who is all in all. There is only one "end all," God in whom all things find their true end and fulfillment. The "be all and end all" of my identity, the real self of my self, is the One "be all and end all," who is Christ.

"I have been crucified with Christ; and it is no longer I who live, but it is Christ who lives in me" (Gal. 2:19-20). To live in hope is to know that I am who I am becoming. Christ in me makes continual space for newness within me. Hope is potency, hope is strenuousness, hope is energy.

> To them God chose to make known how great among the Gentiles are the riches of the glory of this mystery, which is Christ in you, the hope of glory. It is he whom we proclaim, warning everyone and teaching everyone in all wisdom, so that we may present everyone mature in Christ. For this I toil and struggle with all the energy that he powerfully inspires within me. (Col. 1:27-29)

Yet hope is not romantic; it is what energizes when there is nothing human to go on. There is creation by God *ex nihilo*, out of nothing. We are co-creators with God of a future in hope. We create out of nothing, when good outcomes cannot be expected, when there are no grounds for optimism, when, from the human point of view, our personal lives and the life of our society seem certain to go to waste or to hell. Hope cannot be represented as grand or secure, only as something vulnerable, even fragile.

This is what our Christian poets of the twentieth century have been telling us. A memorable image for hope is given by Christopher Fry in *The Lady's Not for Burning:*

> Nothing can be seen
> In the thistle-down, but the rough-head thistle comes.
> Rest in that riddle. I can pass to you
> Generations of roses in this wrinkled berry.
> There: now you hold in your hand a race
> Of summer gardens, it lies under centuries
> Of petals. What is not, you have in your palm.
> Rest in that riddle: why not?[1]

Similar images occur and recur in the great meditations on the three virtues in the poetry of Charles Péguy. Hope is the little bud, the easily-overlooked, the fragile:

> From it everything comes. Without a bud which had once come forth, the tree would not exist. Without these thousands of buds which come forth only once, at the very beginning of April and perhaps in the last days of March, nothing would last....Every life springs from tenderness....
>
> And I tell you, God says, without that burgeoning at the end of April, without those thousands, without that unique little burgeoning of hope, which obviously everybody can break, without that tender downy bud, which the first comer can nip off with his nail, all my creation would be nothing but dead wood.[2]

Notes

1. Christopher Fry, *The Lady's Not for Burning* (New York: Oxford University Press, 1950), 55.

2. Charles Péguy, *The Mystery of the Holy Innocents & Other Poems,* trans. Pansy Pakenham (London: The Harvill Press, 1956), 72-73.

Love

A t the heart of all religion with which rationalism has not tampered there lies a deep sense of mystery and complexity. "The gods love the obscure and hate the obvious," says a key verse of the Upanishads. The religious spirit has expressed itself everywhere in riddles and mazes and koans. Shrines and sacred places are rarely open-plan; instead there are approaches, porches, narthexes, and then various forms of screens. The inner sanctum can only be attained by passing through barriers. The modern, western notion that God can be described (and described simply!), that religion can be summed up in a few plain ideas accessible to all, is one of our more bizarre prejudices.

"Wait a minute!" I can almost hear someone protest at what appears to suggest mystification and elitism. "Didn't Jesus sum up the law and the prophets in a nutshell for everyone in the plain double commandment? 'Hear, O Israel; the Lord our God, the Lord is One. You shall love the Lord your God with all your heart, and with all your soul, and with all your mind and with all your strength. The second is this, You shall love your neighbor as yourself.'" Now I want to prove to you that this double commandment is one of Christianity's most taxing riddles, after the cross itself. Compared with this, the Zen koan about the sound of one hand clapping is almost tame.

First, the very idea that love can be commanded is more than provocative; it seems to border on the absurd. A superior power can command obedience, provided it has sufficient sanctions to enforce. A coercive system can compel conformity, provided rebellion brings down unpleasant consequences. But love is the devotion of the heart. It is a free gift by definition. If God were conceived as a superior power, then yes, God could command service and order obedience—but never love.

So what is the clue to the puzzle? If you read between the lines, God is saying something like this: "Look, if you really knew who I am, the intensity of my beauty, the allure of my glory, the attraction of my love, you would be totally caught up in love. But the trouble is, you would hold back. You would disqualify yourself. You would ridicule yourself for presuming to think that you could be my lover. So I have to tell you, I have to command you! Come to me! Don't hold back! Don't settle for obedience, for religious observance, for conformity! Let yourself go. Go the whole way! Love me! Nothing less will satisfy my love for you!"

It is the saints who have broken the riddle and have passed on the answer to us. Our founder, Father Benson, handed the clue to us when he prayed, "To love Thee were too great a delight even to think of, unless I knew it as a necessity." We wouldn't dare love God unless we were told that it was all right—more than all right, essential, if we are to satisfy God's desire for mutuality in love. The commandment is the expression of God's longing for reciprocal love. God appreciates obedience, but that is nowhere near enough for God's heart.

The commandment is addressed to the *reticent* human heart, not the rebellious heart. Our reticence feeds on a most intractable tendency we have to misapply human categories to God. We tend to treat God as if he or she were a very powerful, even very versatile person, whom we might be lucky to "get to know" but who is most unlikely to want us—ordinary, stupid us—as members of the inner circle of friends. We tend to treat God as one who can only give us a bit of attention some of the time, because there are better people, more urgent affairs that deserve attention. But this is grotesquely anthropomorphic. God is not a finite person; God is Love, wholly present to each and to all.

Wherever you have God, you have all of God. God is entirely and totally available to me as if I were the only being in the world and we had all the time in the world. And at the same instant God is available to you as if you were the only person in the world. The commandment to love God with all our heart, all our soul, all our mind urges us to come right to the front and boldly assume the role of God's lover without shame and without comparing ourselves with others. It is God's way of urging us to be supremely audacious in the way we experience our relationship with God.

Of course, all this is a tremendous challenge to our conventional notions of love. The great commandment is so familiar to us by now that it makes us yawn. The contempt bred by familiarity protects us from having to accept that love is not the bond established between equals, between those who are alike. It is so easy to think that love is the comfortable relationship we have with someone who is our sort of person. Yet that is not really true of the authentic passion of human love. How many marvels are there of marriages and partnerships between extremely unlike people, unlike with an unlikeness that goes far beyond slick language about complementarity!

There is a very telling moment in Christopher Isherwood's novel *The World in the Evening* in which the writer, who as a homosexual might most cherish the notion that love is for connecting like to like, has learned something important.

No, that's not how it begins—not by two people being drawn together. It's the moment when they suddenly know they're different from each other. Utterly, utterly, different; so that it's horribly painful—unbearable almost. You're like the North and South Poles. You couldn't possibly be further apart. And yet, at the same time, you're more connected than any other two points on the surface of the earth. Because there's this axis between you. And everything else turns round it.[1]

The commandment defines love as the mutual relationship between the Creator and the human being. Love is the axis connecting the utterly unlike. Ourselves—mortal, wavering, fragile, half-blind, brilliant and courageous by fits and starts, yet full of fear—and God, the infinitely vital, endlessly compassionate Giver of Life who pervades and surrounds all things, the God who is our source, our companion as Jesus Christ, and the indwelling Spirit. Never mind how unlike God the Trinity we feel now, for we shall feel all the more unlike God the closer we get, so the saints tell us. Unlikeness has nothing to do with it. We can love, though.

Now we move into the second stage of the riddle. The philosopher Charles Hartshorne has written about the Lord's summary of the law:

> There can be few more emphatic utterances in the world's literature. Four times over in one short sentence, the phrase "with all thy" is reiterated. *Nothing* of ourselves is to be withheld; we are to have no devotion, appreciation, concern or interest that is not directed to the divine.[2]

Now anyone who has ever taught a confirmation class is familiar with the very obvious objection, "Who can live like that? And if all our love is to go to God, how can there be anything left over to love our neighbors or ourselves? If God gets all, what is left for ourselves, our neighbors, and the world?" There the riddle stands and we are baffled until the moment of enlightenment.

That moment comes when we realize that God claims all the love of our whole heart because God is all-encompassing and all-embracing, penetrating and pervading all things. God is not one object of love among many. God is the one Lovable One, in and through all things. All loving has God as its ultimate goal. The command to love our neighbor as ourselves spells out some of the implications of the command to love God with all our hearts.

If God is the all-inclusive Reality, then how could we be loving that reality if we failed to love ourselves? We love ourselves precisely because the supremely Lovable One dwells in us and is with us. When we love ourselves truly, we are simply joining God and being with God, like God, toward ourselves.

As for our neighbor, what is lovable about our neighbor, let alone the ultimate stranger, our enemy? How can we *love* our neighbor, not merely tolerate and accommodate? Only by the faith that recognizes there is no such thing as our neighbor or our enemy. Just as there is no such person as myself, only myself and the supremely lovable mystery—God—who dwells in and with me, so there is no such person as my neighbor. There is only my neighbor and the mysterious stranger, the Lovable Other who dwells in and with my neighbor.

To love my enemy and my neighbor is to believe that God is in them and to carry through with that love, even though God's presence is completely hidden. Those who love their neighbor have been enlightened by the realization of a supreme irony that we can express simply like this. If the supremely Lovable One is found in that most implausible of dwellings, that most obscure manger and stable, my own heart, then God must surely be everywhere and must equally be loved everywhere, even in the thickest of disguises, the strangest of incognitos in our unappealing neighbor, our revolting enemy.

Notes

1. Christopher Isherwood, *The World in the Evening* (New York: Avon Books, 1978), 83.

2. Charles Hartshorne, "A Philosopher's Assessment of Christianity," in *Religion and Culture: Essays in Honor of Paul Tillich*, ed. W. Leibrecht (London: SCM, 1958), 167.

Cowley Publications is a ministry of the Society of St. John the Evangelist, a religious community for men in the Episcopal Church. Emerging from the Society's tradition of prayer, theological reflection, and diversity of mission, the press is centered in the rich heritage of the Anglican Communion.

Cowley Publications seeks to provide books, audio cassettes, and other resources for the ongoing theological exploration and spiritual development of the Episcopal Church and others in the body of Christ. To this end, it is dedicated to developing a new generation of theological writers, encouraging them to produce timely, creative, and stimulating publications of excellence, and making these publications available widely, reaching both clergy and lay persons.